Waiting by the Brook

Seven Steps to Deeper Intimacy with God

Kathy-Ann C. Hernandez, Ph.D.

House in the Woods Ministries

To my husband Mark, who unselfishly opened up space in our lives for me to write this book.

To my daughters Alyssa and Amya.
I pray that you will continue to grow into strong women of faith who know what it means to wait patiently on God.

Contents

About this Book

I did not plan to write this book, yet I now know that this is a book that I had to write. If the title captured your attention and you are in search of an in-depth study on the life of the prophet Elijah, please look elsewhere. This book is not primarily about Elijah. It is about waiting on God during uncertain times—during difficult times—during brook experiences, and the steps we can take to benefit the most from these relational encounters.

I invite you to skip to "The Journey Ahead" section or head straight to the "Prologue" if you want to get into the message quickly. However, if you would like to know more about how I came to write this book and why, keep on reading.

In the Spring of 2020, life as we had known it for many years came to an abrupt stop. On March 16, the Governor of Pennsylvania ordered a shutdown of the entire state in a preemptive effort to halt the spread of the novel Coronavirus (COVID-19). At the time, I was in the middle of a busy semester of teaching, but I had already started the mid-semester mental descent in eager anticipation of the slower pace of summer. I was especially looking forward to having blocks of time to work on a book project for which I had a contracted publisher, but for which I had only been able to attack in small bits. Between my work, church, and family commitments, time for focused writing was often the last thing on my to-do-list. The year before, I had applied for a sabbatical to complete the book, but my application had been denied. I was still upset about the denial, but I was determined that once the semester ended I would get the book done. A denied sabbatical was not going to stop me! No way! Then the global pandemic struck, and life changed drastically.

In the midst of the pandemic, my proverbial plate was overflowing with even more commitments: a readjusted teaching schedule, supporting and encouraging overwhelmed graduate students through this new reality, administrative work, church leadership responsibilities, and now facilitating cyber and homeschooling for our children. It seemed that once again circumstances were conspiring to stymie efforts to get that book done. I could not believe it! However, as we waited at home, isolated from relatives and friends, I recalibrated and came up with a different plan: I was going to wake up two hours earlier and work on the book first thing in the mornings.

On one such morning as I sat at my desk to begin writing, a strange thing happened. My mind turned to a sermon I had preached a few months back. In that sermon, entitled simply, "Waiting," I reflected on the life of David and his long journey from shepherd to king. When I was preparing that message, I realized almost immediately that the sermon was really meant for me; it was a not so gentle reminder from God that He was still God, and that I needed to continue to wait on Him.

The message was timely. Since 2015, it had seemed to me as though God was taking me through the wringer with one "loss" after another in my life. The denied sabbatical had just been the bookend to a long string of such losses. At the time, I was perplexed trying to make sense of the many challenges I was facing. I was still in the waiting spot and complaining to God about the injustice of it all. However, preparing that sermon gave me clarity about the waiting experience in a way that I had not understood it before. After I preached, I got confirmation from church members and visitors that the message had resonated with them. Someone even came up to me and said, "That word was for me." But more than the affirmation I received from others, was the quiet confirmation in my spirit that God had used me to comfort others during their season of waiting.

That morning as I sat at my computer, with another academic book to write that would decorate my CV, I realized that God was not finished teaching me about what it means to wait on Him. There was more to learn. I realized also that this message about "waiting on God" needed to be shared with others. In that moment, I laid aside my other book project. Instead, I opened the sermon notes on my computer, and I began writing this book. The sermon itself was about ten pages of written notes, so I quickly googled "chap books" and "eBooks." I decided I was going to write a 10,000-word e-book and get it out before the end of summer. Well, 10,000 words turned into 15,000 and then 30,000 and then 40,000 and now the book that you have in front of you.

As a professor, I am not new to writing for publication. Over the course of my career, I have written and published many articles, book chapters and even co-edited books. Even though I enjoy writing, I will be the first to admit that writing well is hard work. Yet, as I was writing this book, I have felt God's leading and directing. I began jumping out of bed in the morning anxious to get to my desk to write. Getting the first draft done was the easy part. The harder part was formatting, revising and editing the final product that you have in your hand right now.

My intent in writing this book, *Waiting by the Brook: Seven Steps to Deeper Intimacy with God*, is to enter into a conversation with you about what it means to wait on God. Beginning with the experiences of the prophet Elijah, and drawing from my own experiences and the accounts of other Bible characters, I illustrate how waiting on God is critical to our deepening relationship with Him. In fact, the expression "waiting on God" is a term that best describes our positioning in relation to our Maker. We must learn to wait *on* and *with* Him.

In the book of 1 Kings in the Old Testament, we are introduced to the prophet Elijah, who God told to go and wait on Him beside the brook Cherith. Elijah waits there, hidden away during a time of famine, until God reveals his next assignment to him.

The image of this man of God sitting beside a brook waiting

on God fascinates me. I empathize with Elijah. For the last several years, as I have tried to deal with the uncertainty I felt in my own life personally and professionally, this image has become dear to me. In fact, whenever anyone who was interested in my honest response asked the question, "How are you doing?" I would answer simply, "I am waiting by the brook."

The Journey Ahead

Waiting by the Brook begins with a prologue and ends with an epilogue, and it is divided into four main parts. In Part 1, I discuss the challenge we have with waiting and what it means to wait on God. Using the brook Cherith as a metaphor for waiting periods in our developing relationship with God, I reflect on the experiences of Elijah as he waited on God and what these experiences reveal to us about our own brook moments. Part 2, is an account of my personal journey through past waiting periods, an examination of defining characteristics of such brook experiences, and the paradigm shifts that can come to us as we rely on God to make our way through difficulties in life. At the end of Part 2, I share the seven action steps in waiting. Then in Part 3, I elaborate on each action step that is needed for us to successfully navigate brook experiences. Finally, in Part 4, I discuss the most valuable gifts that God eagerly wants to give those who learn to wait patiently *on* and *with* Him.

In writing this book, I have been intentional in doing two things. First, I have chosen to adopt a conversational tone. The reason for this is simple. For much of my Christian life, I have been in search of honest conversations with others who were not afraid to be transparent about the challenges they faced in continuing to trust God during the dark chapters of their lives. I have wanted more spaces where we could talk freely with each other about our wobbly kind of discipleship—spaces in which we would not be made to feel as though such thoughts should not be spoken. That in choosing to lay bare our sometimes-vacillating love for God, we would be removing the masks that get in the way of real conversations. I see a need to create more and more spaces like these for this generation and the next one. And so, in the following pages, I am creating and holding such a space open to give you an authentic view of my experience as a sister traveler in need of a Savior.

The second thing I have been intentional in doing is to use the narrative form of writing to capture my experiences and those of the Bible characters I describe. In the first instance, I do this because I believe there is power in stories. When told from a first-person perspective, stories are valuable tools in capturing the essence of our lived experiences. Our encounter with God is a personal one. The good news or the Gospel is about our individual experience with Him. I also use stories because it is a great teaching tool. Jesus, the master teacher, used stories to teach deep truths. But there is another more personal reason why I have chosen to use stories. At the core, I am a storyteller. From an early age, I learned to appreciate the art of story by listening to a master storyteller—my grandmother. Every night my sister and I along with our cousins would sit on long wooden benches on her Spanish styled verandah, and she would capture our attention and imagination with her gift of storytelling. I know from experience that stories call us to a deeper level of listening. They invite us to listen with our hearts.

Now if you are anything like me when you are about to read a non-fiction book, and you are tempted to skip the prologue and epilogue or jump around from one chapter to the next, please don't. In addition to the underlying message of what it means to wait on God, the chapters reveal my own journey in learning to do just that. I want you to get to know the author behind the book. I am not just writing this book, I am living it. You will get the most out of the book if you read it in sequence.

Two Prayers

I have written this book during one of the most challenging waiting periods that the world has undergone in decades—

a global pandemic. Even as I, like others, struggled to stay healthy, readjust to the new normal, and manage everything that was coming our way, I chose to make room to write by waking up early in the morning before my family was up. In the quiet of those morning hours, I would spend time with God in prayer and Bible study. However, before I got up off my knees and sat at my desk to write, I prayed two simple prayers. The first was, "God let me be like a pen in your hand." The second prayer was for you. I prayed that one day this book would find you as you were waiting beside your brook, and that you would be encouraged to continue to wait on Him.

Waiting by the Brook

Prologue

The first time I met my mother I was seven.

My sister and I were in the backyard of our next-door neighbors' house. Without the intrusion of a fence, both houses shared a common yard bordered at the front by the village road. Someone had climbed the Julie mango tree, and my sister and I along with other neighborhood children were under it shouting instructions to the climber about which fruits to pick. In the midst of all that noise, one of our neighbor's sons came running from the front of our house towards my sister and me. In breathless excitement, he blurted out in spurts, "A woman...out front.... wants to see you... says she is your mother."

"Our mother?" My sister and I looked at each other in confusion. Then the expression on her face changed from confusion to anger, and she promptly ran away. I, on the other hand, as I had done so many nights in my dreams, walked in the direction of this stranger who was my mother; I was ready to enact the long-awaited reunion.

My mother had finally come!

She would explain it all!

I was wrong.

In the much too brief visit that followed, my mother, my sister (who was eventually found and brought back unwillingly), and I sat in our cold, loveless living room—a room without rugs, art work on the walls, dainty trinkets, or a buffet decorated with mementos and family photographs.

She had come to introduce herself. She just wanted to see us. She just wanted to know how we had turned out. There were no answers to the big question that hovered in the air so thick and

1

suffocating that the banal chit chat struggled to make its way through it: Why had she abandoned us?

After a while, a taxi came to pick her up, and my sister and I were left with no answers, no solutions BUT unwanted gifts— two green balloons, and a twenty-five-cent piece that she had given us to share. Yes, to share!

In this visit that is forever etched in my memory, I experienced my earliest and most poignant memory of waiting. I had waited in anticipation of a visit. I had waited in agony during the visit, and I continued to wait long after the visit with unresolved residuals.

I had spent the first seven years and counting of my life waiting for a happy reunion that never came.

A small creek runs by my home. Well, not much of a creek anymore, but I have been told that in years past it was more than its current trickling presence. Now, it is more of a brook that quietly meanders and trickles along over a few larger rocks and fallen debris that litter its path. However, in the early spring or after a heavy downpour, we see glimpses of its former glory as its waters sometimes spill over the bank and threaten to turn our driveway into a natural river way.

When we first moved here, we would walk down to the brook and stand in the shade of the evergreen listening to its soft ripples. Most of my interaction with this brook, though, happens half a mile down from our house. There it joins the flow from other houses and empties its contents into a larger creek that runs alongside a naturally wooded trail. When I am out for my early morning walk, run, or bike ride, I have come to appreciate the creek as a faithful companion with its steady hum of gently flowing water and its familiar array of geese and mallards out for a swim or water fun.

Yet on many mornings, and at the time I started writing this book, I have found my mind at odds with the beauty of the tranquil surroundings. The events of the last four to five years have convinced me that God is allowing me to stay once again in a holding pattern—waiting on Him.

On mornings like these, the flowing water does not soothe, and the squawks of geese, mallards and ducks only annoy. I have to keep reminding myself, "Kathy-Ann live in the present moment!" "Be intentional!" "This moment is your life!" I keep up this internal dialogue with myself, repeating the messages I share weekly on my Facebook v-log[1], "One Minute of Inspiration." But at this moment, I feel like a hypocrite. "What a fraud you are!" I say to myself. "You are peddling stuff that you are not even practicing. C'mon girl, practice what you preach!" Sadly, I am beyond heeding my own advice. Rogue thoughts give me no rest: "When is God going to do what He has promised in my life?" "How much longer must I wait on Him for clarity about my next steps?" Plagued by this internal dialogue, I struggle to allow the calming presence of the stately sycamores and green foliage to quiet my agitated spirit.

I try again to remind myself that certainly I have much for which to be thankful. The Lord has brought me a long way from the living room I sat in as that little girl who waited for a mother to return. I am now a tenured professor. I am married to a wonderful man, and we have two kind-hearted daughters who fill our lives with laughter, messiness, and unforgettable memory making moments. God has been good! He has brought me from very humble beginnings, growing up in a small village in the twin island Republic of Trinidad and Tobago to live here in the suburbs of one of the largest US cities. Our home is nestled in the woods a few feet away from the little brook that runs through the front of our property. What a blessing! I am indeed grateful for it all, and yet, there has settled inside me a quiet discomfort that continues to grow.

The opening story illustrates well that I am not new to waiting. In fact, when I reflect on my life, I can see in the rear view mirror a series of waiting moments. There is, of course, the seven or so years that I waited to meet my mother, and the years after that visit that I kept on hoping and praying to a God I did not even know that she would return. Then at various stages of my life from then to now as a believer in Christ, there have been seasons of waiting. In fact, if there is one word that describes my continuing relationship with God through the highs and lows of life, it would be this: "waiting."

I have waited on God many times for answered prayers. Sometimes He has answered in miraculous ways, sometimes He has not. The answers have not always been what I hoped or prayed for, but He has answered. And always, even while I waited in seasons of ambiguity, even though I could not clearly see the path, He was leading me through up ahead, there was God faithfully providing for my current needs. This is the space in which I find myself on this particular morning—waiting on Him.

For the last several years, I have sensed God's calling on my life, but that calling is yet to be fulfilled, and so I wait. I know that He has another assignment for me that will allow me to use the gifts He has been developing in me for the last decade of my life—gifts of leadership, writing, teaching, and speaking. Yet it would seem that every movement I have made to advance in the direction of that calling, I have faced obstacle after obstacle. What looked like open doors have been slammed shut in my face one after one, and so I wait. In this waiting spot, I am puzzled and unsure of my next steps, and so I wait. Why is God keeping from me the very thing that would advance me? Why do I find myself at this season of my life beside a brook with these gifts still hidden inside me and unsure of my next steps?

In spite of the many waiting patterns I have been in over the years, waiting is still difficult.

Part I

Chapter 1. The Problem with Waiting

A Robin's Nest

A few years ago, I was lucky to observe a robin's nest up close. Over the course of the spring and summer, I watched the drama of new life unfolding. I first noticed a very plump robin making endless trips to various spots in the yard; she was collecting leaves and twigs in her beak and bringing them back to the rhododendron shrub that stood to the left of our front porch. It was in the crook of one of the uppermost branches that she kept working her architectural magic. Soon she had crafted a cozy nest. The many trips to collect building supplies ceased. She now spent most of her time sitting on the nest. I found a peeking spot through our living room window, and I waited patiently for her to leave so I could get that first look inside the nest.

One morning as soon as she had flown away, I found my opportunity. Quickly, I made my way out the door and stood on tiptoes with my phone in hand. I raised the phone high above the nest and clicked the camera button a few times. Mama robin looked on suspiciously from a spot in the yard. When I turned the phone around to get a look at the captured image, the beauty of it caught me by surprise. Wow! There nestled between the brown leaves and twigs were three beautiful blue eggs.

That day I began a vigil monitoring the nest. Every morning, like a nosy neighbor, I checked to see if the birds had hatched. Unfortunately, I was scheduled to leave for a trip to Kenya. Just before I left for my trip, I checked the nest again—the eggs were still there. Still, I did not want to miss the grand event altogether, so I left my husband with strict orders to continue the watch and to take pictures while I was away. I suppose it was too much to expect that he would attend to the full extent of my "honey-do-list" and still document the birth of three baby birds. Of course, he missed the entire event! When I returned from my trip two weeks later, the nest was empty. I was disappointed.

However, in July, I was in luck again! I noticed that a robin was back in the nest. Was it the same bird? I could not tell. But sure enough, there she was sitting diligently on the nest. When I was able to get a photo, there were four eggs in the nest this time. And so, I began a new vigil. But once again, it was summer break and the entire family was headed out for a month-long road trip. I kept hoping that this time the eggs would hatch before we left. I got my wish! The eggs hatched. Every morning before we left, I stood on the tip of my toes again and angled my camera phone well above the nest to get a look at the hatchlings—little balls of flesh with a smattering of grey feathers randomly stuck on lay crammed inside the nest. That was the last look I got. By the time we returned from our trip, the nest was empty again.

I was fascinated by this birthing cycle. I wanted to learn more, so to Google I went. I learned that the incubation period for birds varies by type. For example, robins incubate for about 12-14 days on average before they hatch. It takes about 2 weeks for the birds to first venture from the nest, or "fledge," and shortly after they leave. How's that for a quick turnaround from infancy to adulthood! In contrast, eagles like the golden eagle take about 40-45 days to hatch and about 7-11 weeks to fledge. The bald eagle takes about 35 days to hatch and eaglets fledge at 10-14 weeks. Interesting, isn't it?

We have different waiting periods for two of the same species—birds. Both destined to fly. Both going through a similar maturation period—from egg to hatchling, to nestling, to fledgling and then to adult bird. And yet, one has to *wait* 4 to 6 times as long as the other to advance towards its destiny.

A Problem with Waiting

I don't know about you, but I don't do very well with waiting for something or someone. In fact, if I am honest, I can become downright impatient, resentful even when I have to wait, especially when I look to my right or to my left and I see that someone just like me is moving right along at a good and steady pace.

I have a problem with waiting for something as simple as checking out at the supermarket. Often, before choosing my checkout line, I survey the territory. I look at each cashier and how quickly or slowly they are working. Sometimes I do a quick count of the number of items in the shopping cart of each customer in line; I also count the number of customers in the line. Armed with this critical information, I choose the line with the greatest probability of getting me in and out as quickly as possible. But even after all of that, I become irritated when I find that the line to the right or left of me is now moving faster than the line I chose.

More to the point, I often struggle to wait patiently on God. There have been too many times when I have become impatient waiting on Him to move in response to something that I have been praying about sometimes for weeks, months and even years. I get a bit upset, even angry when God seems silent and things are taking a long time to happen. The waiting is all the more unbearable, when I act in accordance with God's promises to me: "Kathy-Ann, I have great plans to prosper you to give you hope and a good future."[2] So what do I do? I step forward in faith. I submit my job application. I go through the phone interview process, prepare for the job talk, deliver the job talk, and then I still don't get the job! What gives, God? Sometimes I cry out to Him, "Are you there?" "Are you listening?" "How much longer must I wait for you to do what you promised?" Can I just admit that I have a problem with waiting?

In Good Company

I know that I am not the only one who struggles through the waiting. In fact, I suspect that the reason you picked up this book is because like me, you recognize these waiting patterns in your own life. Perhaps my opening story resonates with you because right now you find yourself in such a pattern that is testing your faith. What do you do while you are waiting on God? How should you wait?

There is a paradox of living through a waiting period. On the one hand, we are admonished to live gratefully in the present, while on the other hand we are encouraged to have great expectations for the future. Although there is much to be thankful for, there is also much to hope for. How do we live joyfully in the wait?

When we read about the lives of many other men and women of faith in the Bible—Abraham, Sarah, Joseph, Jacob, Paul, Hannah, and David—we see that during their walk with God, they too were held in waiting patterns. Then there is the prophet Elijah who also spent much time waiting on God.

How did Elijah navigate this period of uncertainty in his life? How did he do it? Though I can only imagine the emotions Elijah felt during this time, I find comfort in knowing that even this great man of God had to wait for a season. He had to wait beside a brook that would soon dry up.

The Prophet Elijah

In the book of Kings, we are introduced to Elijah the prophet. Elijah arrives on the scene without preamble. We do not know much about his background other than what is recorded there: *"And Elijah the Tishbite who was of the inhabitants of Gilead said unto Ahab, As the Lord God of Israel, liveth, before whom I stand, there shall not be dew or rain these years, but according to my word."*[3]

What an entrance! This relatively "unknown man" has an encounter with the king, Ahab, and he delivers a bold and startling message from God. But the real story begins after this meeting. God tells the prophet to go hide himself beside a brook and wait.

King Ahab of the Northern Kingdom

The context in which this encounter takes place is important to the story that unfolds. Ahab was king of the Northern Kingdom of Israel which became involved in idol worship after the nation of Israel divided into two separate kingdoms—the Northern and Southern kingdoms. The children of Israel were God's chosen people with a sovereign ruler—God. However, when they insisted on an earthly king, God gave them King Saul. But King Saul's actions soon showed that he was not willing to follow God's leading, so God sent the prophet Samuel to anoint a young shepherd boy, David, to be the next king of Israel. King David committed many sins in his life for which he repented and, in spite of these and other missteps, he remained faithful to God.

After David's death, his son, Solomon became king. King Solomon's early reign was marked by devotion to God and a reliance on Him to rule wisely. However, in later years King Solomon allowed idol worship into Israel and burdened the people with heavy taxes. Tension among the twelve tribes of Israel grew. Solomon's successor, his son Rehoboam, instituted even harsher taxes. This was when the nation of Israel split— 10 tribes left the Kingdom of Judah and formed the Northern Kingdom and the remaining tribes (the tribes of Judah and Benjamin) formed the Southern Kingdom. The Northern Kingdom included a long succession of kings including Ahab who all "*did evil in the sight of the LORD.*"[4] But King Ahab was considered to be the worst of them all, and his wife Jezebel is also infamous for being wicked.[5] It was King Ahab who introduced the Canaanite god, Baal, to the children of Israel. Baal was believed to be the god of rain, wind, and fertility: "*He (Ahab) set up an altar for Baal in the temple of Baal, which he had built in Samaria. And Ahab made a wooden image. Ahab did more to provoke the LORD God of Israel to anger than all the kings of Israel who were before him."*[6] Elijah's entrance onto the scene to deliver a message from the one true God was as much about God's judgment on this wicked king, as it was about a confrontation between the only God who controls the rain and the false god Baal which King Ahab had introduced to God's people.

The Prophet and the King

Many things are striking about this meeting between Elijah the prophet and King Ahab. The first is that though we can easily trace the lineage of King Ahab by reading a few chapters back, we know very little about Elijah's background. Ahab is the seventh king of the Northern kingdom of Israel. Evil though he may be, he comes from a long line of kings all infamous for being evil. On the other hand, Elijah comes with no such illustrious ancestry. We are told simply that he is a Tishbite. Elijah's actual lineage is uncertain. Some Bible scholars suggest that the title "Elijah the Tishbite" is probably given to him to describe his birthplace Tishi—believed to be somewhere in Gilead where Elijah dwelt among the people. However, some translations of the original Hebrew of this term, "Tishbite," interpret the word as having the same meaning as the word "inhabitants"; it means a "stranger." The verse then reads: *"Elijah the stranger from among the strangers in Gilead."*[7] Even though the details of his ancestry may remain a mystery, there is one thing that is certain about Elijah. He is a man of God. His name is his most valuable calling card—Elijah's name means, "Yahweh is my God".

The second thing that is striking about Elijah's encounter with King Ahab is that after he delivers this prophetic message, he disappears. How anticlimactic! If we were expecting an extended confrontation—a one-on-one show down in which the prophet would be able to flex his spiritual muscles, we are disappointed. What! Shouldn't Elijah be putting his ministry into full gear, going door to door and speaking to God's people? Isn't this his big ministry debut? Apparently not!

Elijah Waits on God

God's hiding of Elijah during this time shows God's punishment on the people for their sins. Since the prophet was God's mouthpiece to the children of Israel, withdrawing Elijah's ministry symbolized God drawing away His presence from them. But is there more going on here than God's punishment for His people? Yes, there is! Elijah's time in hiding is also about what God is going to do in Elijah as he waits. Elijah hides away not because he is afraid, but because God directs him to do so. *"And the word of the Lord came unto him, saying. Get thee hence, and turn thee eastward and hide thyself by the brook Cherith, that is before Jordan."*[8]

It is here at the brook that Elijah must wait on God to give him his next assignment. But hadn't God already given the prophet the original assignment to go and confront King Ahab? So now that Elijah has diligently followed the word of God, he has to wait before he can continue his ministry as a prophet? Really? I wonder how Elijah must have felt. Prophets were God's messengers to the people. Elijah's gift was to be God's spokesperson to the children of Israel. I imagine that Elijah was good at what he did, and that is why God had chosen him. However, at this critical point of his ministry, God sends him to hide beside a brook.

This waiting period is further marked by uncertainty. It is during this time that we see this man of God with a message bound up inside him but lacking an audience. His audience is a makeshift crew of wildlife and, eventually, a widow and her son. This period is characterized by God's faithfulness in providing enough for Elijah. Beside the brook Cherith, God sends ravens to feed him, and he drinks fresh flowing water. While adequate, there is much that is perplexing about the provisions that God chooses to give Elijah. In Jewish tradition, ravens were unclean birds and the Jews were told to avoid them as unclean meat. Still God chose these unclean birds to be the prophet's food messengers. As if that were not enough, the brook from which Elijah drinks daily, begins to dwindle from a small stream to a trickle, and then the water stops altogether. The brook dries up! When the brook dries up, the word of the Lord comes to him again with his next assignment: *"And the word of the Lord came unto him, saying, Arise, get thee to Zarephath which belongeth to Zidon, and dwell there: behold, I have commanded a widow woman there to sustain thee."*[9]

Following God's command, Elijah arrives at the gates of the village, and there he sees a widow gathering sticks. He asks her for some water and a little bread for God has promised that this woman would feed him. But alas, this is not the beginnings of the bountiful feast that the prophet might have anticipated. Instead, the widow tells him that all the food she has left is a last bit of flour in a jar and a little cooking oil. Elijah listens to the voice of God and tells the widow to prepare bread for him first and then for her son: *"The God of Israel, says: There will always be flour and olive oil left in your containers until the time when the LORD sends rain and the crops grow again!"*[10] And it happens just as God has said.

God leads Elijah first to a palace to confront a king, then on to a hiding spot beside a brook, and then to rest in the house of a widow and her son, as Elijah waits on God for his next assignment. In every circumstance, we see God continuing to faithfully provide for his servant. The provisions are not bountiful, but they are just enough. Elijah has what he needs to survive this phase of his journey, but still he must wait on God to direct his next steps.

Waiting on God

Like the prophet Elijah or like other faithful men and women in the Bible, have you been waiting on God? Have you been persisting in prayer, fasting, petitioning God for what He has promised you? Have you been waiting for a long time while it seems to you that others you know are moving along at a good pace? Perhaps God has already given you the answer, but now you are waiting for the promise to be fulfilled? Are you now in that place where you are getting a bit tired and frustrated with waiting?

If this is you, I can empathize with how you might be feeling. Even though waiting on God is an inextricable part of our relationship with Him as followers, just like it was for the patriarchs of old, "waiting on God" is one of the activities that challenges us the most. We don't enjoy waiting. We can begin to doubt God while we wait. We can become frustrated with this period of perceived inactivity, and we can even decide to abandon the wait altogether.

But what if far from being a state of dormancy, the waiting period is actually one of the most active periods of the Christian journey? What if it is in the experience of waiting patiently on God that we are best positioned to receive the most customized gifts that God eagerly wants to give us?

There is a paradox of living through a waiting period. On the one hand, we are admonished to live gratefully in the present, while on the other hand we are encouraged to have great expectations for the future.

Chapter 2. Waiting by the Brook

A Prophet in Waiting

The image of Elijah waiting by a brook is a study in contrasts. There is something calming about being next to a brook. The sound of water trickling over rocks as it meanders along is soothing, comforting, inspiring even. Yet, here is Elijah by the brook Cherith awaiting his next assignment from God. Is it possible that in the midst of this waterside respite, fears, and anxieties threaten to disrupt his calm?

On the one hand, because of his relationship with God, Elijah can be certain that God will take care of him, but on the other hand he is also occupying a space of uncertainty about the next steps in his ministry and calling as a prophet. It was Elijah who had prayed for the drought with hopes that the people would return to God.[11] But now that his prayers have been answered, how is he coping mentally and emotionally?

While he sits by the brook being fed by ravens, all around him the nation is experiencing a famine. In case you read over that word *famine* too quickly, pause for a minute and consider the suffering that is contained in that word. Famines were often so very severe that sometimes people would eat anything they could find including wild vines, heads of animals, garbage, dung and we are told even human flesh.[12] Is Elijah concerned about the people and their suffering? Is he concerned about his own fate? Is he wondering about how long the water in the brook will continue to flow or about what God will call him to do next? How long must he continue to wait on God to open up a pathway for him to continue his active work as a prophet—God's messenger to the people? How prepared is Elijah to wait on God?

Understanding the Wait

From my earliest memories, Psalm 27 has been one of my favorite psalms. At a young age, my mind fixated on the verse: *"Even if my father and mother abandon me, the Lord will hold me close."*[13] What a wonderful promise! However, this well-known psalm does not only offer words of comfort for those who are abandoned, it also ends with guidance about what needs to happen for us to receive this kind of comfort from God: *"Wait on the Lord, be of good courage and He will strengthen thine heart. Wait I say on the Lord."*[14] The psalmist counsels us to *wait* on God. But what does it mean to wait on God?

In everyday use, we understand the word *"wait"* to mean that we remain where we are or we delay some action that we intend to take until a set time or until something else happens. The person who is waiting in effect relinquishes control of the outcome and/or delays action for some reason that is either in their control or outside of their control. For instance, I may choose to wait until after dinner to have a cookie because I want to enjoy my dinner first. I could also wait until I am sixteen to get my US driver's license because the law of the land says that is when I can legally obtain one. In the first case, I am in control of the wait; in the latter, I am not.

In our relationship with God *waiting* takes on a more nuanced meaning. The Hebrew word The psalmist uses for "wait" is "qavah". It means "to wait, look for, hope, expect." Albert Barnes, a well-respected theologian and Bible commentator, offers the following notes on this passage:

> Wait on the Lord—This is the sum of all the instruction in the psalm; the main lesson which the psalm is designed to convey. The object is to induce others, from the experience of the psalmist, to *trust*

in the Lord; to *rely upon Him;* to *come to Him in trouble and danger;* to *wait for His interposition when all other resources fail....*in all times of danger and difficulty, instead of despondency, *instead of sinking down in despair, instead of giving up all effort, we should go forward in the discharge of duty, putting our trust solely in the Lord.*[15]

I have italicized several key phrases here, which I encourage you to re-read and to meditate on the implications of these phrases in the context of your relationship with God. When I read the passage with these phrases in mind, I realize that to wait on God is to *relinquish any control that I think I may have over the situation, and to leave it solely in His capable hands.* However, there is also an underlying implication which you might miss altogether. Waiting on God is a very active state of being. It is described here with multiple verb and verb phrases: "we trust," "we rely upon," "we come to Him in trouble," "we choose to not give up," and "we should go forward"! We wait! If we do this, we can expect God to strengthen us as the psalmist says here.

As I have continued to walk with God through the years, I have returned to this Psalm 27 time and time again as I found myself hidden beside my own brooks. In fact, the Christian path is made up of several Cherith brook experiences. It can happen while we are waiting for an answer to our prayers, even after God has heard and answered our prayers, or after the promise has been fulfilled in our lives.

Waiting for an Answer

When we bring a request before God for something that we desperately want or need, we often find ourselves in a waiting spot. This is the place where we wait in expectation that God will move in response to our prayers. Sometimes the answer "yes" comes swiftly; but other times the answers are a long time in coming. Sometimes the answers are not exactly what we had prayed for, and sometimes God answers "no."

Waiting for answers to prayers tests our patience. Moreover, God's response to us is specific to our needs and unique circumstances. For example, as I will explore in more detail in Chapter 8, when Hannah prayed persistently for a son, God granted her request. However, King David's petition for God to save the life of his first-born son was not granted: *"David begged God to spare the child. He went without food and lay all night on the bare ground. The elders of his household pleaded with him to get up and eat with them, but he refused. Then on the seventh day the child died."*[16]

The examples of Hannah and David illustrate how God's responses are individually customized. His responses are not arbitrary. We can and should come to God with our requests. And yes, we may not always get what we prayed for; we may not even understand the reason behind the answer He gives. Yet God invites us into a deepening relationship with Him as we wait for the answer to our prayers. In fact, waiting on God for an answer to our prayers is as much about bringing our requests before Him as it is about starting a conversation. It is in the process of conversing that we can begin to understand Him and His will for our life. This is the meeting place where we have an opportunity to bring our will in alignment with His larger purpose. The *Amplified Bible* puts it this way: *"And this is the confidence (the assurance, the privilege of boldness) which we have in Him: [we are sure] that if we ask anything (make any request) according to His will (in agreement with His own plan), He listens to and hears us."*[17] Presenting our requests to God then is only the beginning of that conversation.

Waiting in the Answer

Even when God answers our prayers, there is often an interval in which we must continue to wait on Him. In this space, we are challenged to believe that what He has promised, He will fulfill. At the brook Cherith, Elijah finds himself continuing a conversation with God after he had already received the answer "yes" to his prayers asking God for a famine in the land. God had further instructed Elijah to go and confront King Ahab, but after the encounter with the king, God tells the prophet to go sit by the brook and wait. Elijah is waiting in the answer to his prayers.

There are two things about waiting by the brook Cherith that are important to note. First, there is something that is unsettling about the circumstances in which God chooses to hide the prophet. Elijah is sent to hide first beside a brook that soon dries up, and next at the house of a widow who is about to run out of food. A brook can be described as a ravine that is dry except in the rainy season. Notice, it is not a mighty river with heavy flowing water, but a ravine. According to *Merriam Webster Dictionary*, a ravine is "a small narrow steep-sided valley... that is usually worn by running water." Why does God place Elijah beside this trickling flow of water that is about to dry up? There is nothing to drink here, except for the water that flows from the brook. There is nothing to eat here except what God sends him via ravens.

During the period of waiting, first beside the brook and later at the widow's house, Elijah's sustenance comes solely through the provisions of God. He has to come to a place as he waits in the answer to his prayers, where he is fully depending on God —where he is living on God. Pastor Colin Smith, Senior Pastor of The Orchard Evangelical Free Church, in an inspiring sermon titled "When God Hides You," puts it this way: "To live on God who is invisible means to find what you need in God when there isn't anything or anyone else."[18]

Secondly, this is not an ordinary brook. The word *Cherith* comes from the Hebrew verb, *karat*, which means "to corral together up and cut off." God leads Elijah to this place of isolation where he is cut off from the people in his ministry, and he is totally dependent on God. Why has God positioned the prophet in this place of hiding at this time? Why has he chosen to keep the prophet hidden beside a brook? What appeared to be the great launching of Elijah's ministry after a word from God himself, turns into an extended waiting period.

Elijah's experience here, as well as the experiences of many other Bible characters suggests to us that preparation is needed before God can accomplish His great work in our lives. The Cherith experience then, can be that place in our journey where we know we are in alignment with God's will for our life, and yet he tells us to wait. Colin Smith describes *Cherith* this way:

> Cherith is the place where God withholds what you wanted most. Cherith is the place where God closes the door on what you wanted to do for him. . . It comes to every Christian at some point in their journey.[19]

At Cherith, God chooses to hide Elijah for a season. Here Elijah must wait patiently and trust that God will indeed do what He has promised.

Waiting After the Answer

Elijah remains in hiding for about three years until God allows him to walk back into the public ministry to which he had been called. An unforgettable ministerial climax comes after this season of hiding. Elijah faces King Ahab again and has a confrontation on Mount Carmel with the prophets of Baal against God. In one of the most dramatic and entertaining showdowns in the Old Testament, Elijah challenges the idolatrous king and his prophets to a contest to see whose God can call down fire from heaven to burn up a sacrifice. The prophets of Baal try for hours with no success. When it is Elijah's turn, he "ups the ante" by soaking the sacrifice in gallons of water. Then Elijah calls on his God, and God responds swiftly sending down fire from heaven that completely consumes the sacrifice. But God's triumph through His prophet is not over. On Elijah's command, the people seize the prophets of Baal and kill them all. Elijah then goes to the top of Mount Carmel and prays to God to send down rain: "*And soon the sky was black with clouds. A heavy wind brought a terrific rainstorm, and Ahab left quickly for Jezreel.*"[20]

However, shortly after Carmel, we find Elijah going into hiding again. Elijah is afraid of what the king's wife, Jezebel, will do to him when she learns about what he has done, so he runs away. He is so despondent that he eventually sits under a juniper tree and asks God to take his life. But a merciful God sends an angel to take care of the cowardly prophet once again. God provides Elijah with *"bread baked on hot stones and a jar of water."*[21] Elijah eats and is able to travel a forty-day journey until he comes to a cave where he spends the night.

Once again, the prophet is in hiding. In this instance though, he is hiding not because God has sent him into hiding, but because he has fallen victim to relying on his own strength to be effective. Even though Elijah makes this crucial mistake, God does not abandon him. Instead, God comes looking for him:

> *"Go out and stand before me on the mountain," the Lord told him. And as Elijah stood there, the Lord passed by, and a mighty windstorm hit the mountain. It was such a terrible blast that the rocks were torn loose, but the Lord was not in the wind. After the wind there was an earthquake, but the Lord was not in the earthquake. And after the earthquake there was a fire, but the Lord was not in the fire. And after the fire there was the sound of a gentle whisper. When Elijah heard it, he wrapped his face in his cloak and went out and stood at the entrance of the cave. And a voice said, "What are you doing here, Elijah?"*[22]

After this encounter with God, Elijah gets even more assignments. God directs him to appoint another king and eventually to appoint his own successor, Elisha. Finally, Elijah's relationship with God has deepened so much during his many waiting experiences that God takes the prophet away in grand style: *"Suddenly a chariot of fire appeared with horses of fire, and separated the two of them; and Elijah went up by a whirlwind into heaven."*[23] God takes Elijah to be with Him forever.

Learning to Wait

The experiences of Elijah illustrate well the waiting patterns that are part of a deepening relationship with God. Before Elijah could stand on Mount Carmel and have the most pivotal experience in his prophetic ministry, he was directed by God to remain in obscurity, sitting by a brook and then waiting at a widow's house. One might assume that Elijah had learned all the lessons he had to learn to continue to effectively fulfill his role as a prophet. He had not. It would take more waiting experiences for Elijah to learn to wait for the answer to his prayers, then to wait in the answer, and finally to wait after the answer. It was through the process of this deepening relationship as He waited on God that Elijah was able to receive the great gift that God had in store for Him—an eternal home with Him.

As you reflect on your life experience can you see familiar waiting patterns? Have there been times when you were asking God to fulfill a desperate need in your life? Were you praying day after day, month after month, perhaps even year after year, but still God seemed silent? Perhaps, God had answered "yes" to your prayers for a husband or a child, the remission from cancer, a job opening, or a recommendation for hire, but you still had to wait for the promise to materialize. Maybe the answer was "no," and like it was for King David, the baby did die. Now you are living in the space of alignment with what God has allowed to happen.

You might be in a place where in spite of how God has worked in your life in the past, you are facing new challenges. Even though God has done miraculous things in your life, you are puzzled by His apparent silence and lack of clarity for your life now. You might have felt God calling you to do a "new thing" or to a new situation but you do not know what that thing is. You may be questioning why you are still stuck in the same job, relationship or position. Even though your bread and water are secure, you feel the call on your life to do more and be more.

Ask me how I know?

My life has been punctuated by a series of these waiting moments: waiting for an answer, then waiting on God *in* the answer, and still waiting after the answer. Brook experiences are not indicative of a specific location in the waiting pattern with God—before, during or after answered prayer. Rather, the brook is a metaphor for the challenges we face in life as we learn to navigate them in full dependence on God. Wherever, we are in the pattern, we must learn to wait on God.

∞∞∞

To wait on God is to relinquish any control that I think I may have over the situation, and to leave it solely in His capable hands.

Part 2

Chapter 3. Waiting Patterns in the Rearview Mirror

Recollecting Past Victories

On most mornings, I get up early and put on my biking or running gear. I follow the brook that runs through our property to a nearby creek that flows alongside a natural park of multi-use trails. It is a tranquil spot to exercise both my mind and body. I love seeing how the trail changes in character from winter, to spring, to summer and fall. On this one particular morning though, I am immune to the beauty around me. I recognize that like Elijah, I am once again at a Cherith experience in my life.

There is much about the prophet Elijah with which I can identify. You see, based on my lineage, there was nothing remarkable about my upbringing that would set me apart. In fact, if there was a poster child for "at risk", it would have been me. I was born and raised in the Caribbean twin island Republic of Trinidad and Tobago, in a single parent household. My journey to this point in my life came through struggle and the mercies of God.

One of my favorite Christian authors, Ellen G. White, wrote these inspiring words in *Christian Experience and Teachings* as she recollected her own journey:

> In reviewing our past history, having traveled over every step of advance to our present standing, I can say, Praise God! As I see what God has wrought, I

am filled with astonishment, and with confidence in Christ as leader. We have nothing to fear for the future, except as we shall forget the way the Lord has led us, and His teaching in our past history. (p. 204.1)

On mornings, like this one, I lean heavily on recollections of past victories in my life. I am desperately in need of inspiration. As I reflect on my life experiences up to this point, what I can see in the rearview mirror is one brook experience after another, and God's faithful provisions through them all.

A Mother who Never Was

I say that I met my mother when I was seven years old, but I don't know exactly how old I was. I can only guess. And yet the memory of that first encounter is very vivid. At the point of her visit, I had been waiting for her for almost all my life.

My mother, I was told, had dropped my sister and me off at our grandmother's house one day with a promise to return. I was just a baby and my sister was almost two years old. When morning turned to evening, and then night, and days turned into weeks, it was clear that she was not coming back. I remember spending my early years trying to form a mental picture of this woman in my mind.

Who was *she*? For many years that is all it was, just *she*. There was no face, no memory, no smell to connect a nine-month bond to the person who bore me and the person I was becoming. All I had were images in my mind glued together from the decrepit comments of others—dimples., short..., black..., young. This was *she*.

She was a desire yet to be fulfilled. In the cold places of my heart there was this wanting to be acknowledged and nurtured, to experience the mother-daughter bond that I read so often of in the Enid Blyton[24] books that crowded my days. Where was the one with whom I could share confidences and silly laughs? Where was the one who would tend to colds and the measles and the mumps, and dry my tears because I cried too much when my dog, Sparky, died? There were no fresh baked cookies shared together or experiments in the kitchen preparing the woman to be in the child.

And so, I waited to be introduced to this woman who had given me birth. I waited for the day that my mother would come and explain it all. She would tell why she dropped me off and never came back. The love that had escaped me in those early years had been stored in the banks of my childhood imagination and naivety; I waited for the day when this fund would be lavished on me.

Well, she did eventually come, but she did not stay. One day as my sister and I were out in our neighbor's backyard with other children picking mangoes, a car pulled up and there she was. The visit was brief. There was no explanation, just meaningless chit-chat none of which I can remember now. She needed to satisfy her curiosity, to see how we had turned out. That was all.

After the visit, the craving for a maternal presence still remained. It was a vacant hole, mysteriously dark and unfulfilled, but still I kept waiting and hoping. So before and even after that visit, I spent my early years looking for acceptance and love to ward off the fear that I was not good enough to be loved. And just below that layer of fear was another one; it was the fear that I did not have what it would take to be a good mother.

But God sent others to mother me. He sent strong and compassionate women who stood in the motherhood gap—women who taught me how to cook, and other women who stepped in to instruct me about womanhood. There was the next-door neighbor who had "the talk" with my dad about what a maturing girl would need and introduced him to the concept of a "bra." There was the family friend who made sure Dad understood that I needed to look right for my high school graduation party. There was the dean of women at the boarding school I attended during my teenage years. Then there was "Mom" (my mother-in-law). All these women and many, many more, nurtured me, loved me, taught me, and shaped me into the woman I am always becoming. They poured into an empty mothering hole till it was overflowing. Yes, God had intervened to fill the motherhood gaps in my life.[25]

Dreams of Higher Education

My father did his best to raise me well. Dad believed that there were two worthy pursuits in life—cultivating a relationship with God and pursuing education. The first did not cost much money—just the cost of the two or three church dresses and one pair of shoes to attend church. He also sent my sister and me to Christian schools. It was in these spaces that I learned about a love that tugged at my unloved heart. My young mind struggled to comprehend a love that would allow a father to send His only son to die for *me*, when my own mother had abandoned *me*. I yearned for a love like that; I wanted more than anything to be enveloped in it.

I remember crying out to God, still praying to Him that my mother would return for me. I did not really know how to pray. Too often the words got swallowed up in tears and sobs. But I stayed often on my knees in the divine embrace of this unseen presence allowing Him to comfort my grieving heart. I was nine years old when I told my father that I wanted to publicly give my heart to God in baptism, but he said I was too young. Then at the age of twelve with his consent, I was baptized.

At the time, my father was not much of a religious man himself, and yet he seemed to value Christian education. From my early education journey in a Christian elementary school, Dad later enrolled my sister and me in a Christian boarding academy which he could barely afford. Though he had not finished high school himself, education beckoned him as a commodity of great value, if not for himself then for his daughters. Even now, I have a fixed image of him driving his green crown Toyota taxi, with a silver angel on the bonnet, back and forth from my home village of Sangre Grande to Matura where our grandmother lived, accepting crumpled dollar bills and loose change, gathering them all up into precious investment bundles to invest in our education. Yet when it came to college, I knew that he would not be able to afford it. And so, I waited on God to make a way for me to be the first in my family to begin the higher education journey.

God did send help! He sent mentors and sponsors to open up doors for me to work my way through a bachelor's degree with a concentration in English, and then on to graduate school to complete a master's degree at a small Christian university in Michigan. But while there, I struggled to pay the tuition. My bills kept rising. Every US dollar that I owed was equal to six Trinidad and Tobago dollars. How would I pay? I waited on God again, and He answered.

Midway through my master's program, I heard of a job opening for instructors in the English Language Department at a Community College in the British Virgin Islands (BVI). Though a British dependent territory, the BVI uses US currency. Getting that job would solve my financial problems. I applied, and I asked God to give me the job. He did! Over the course of the next year, I was able to work and complete my final courses online, return in the following summer to complete my comprehensive exams, and graduate with a master's degree in educational leadership. God had done it again!

Navigating Storms in Paradise

I loved living on Tortola, the largest island in the group of islands that make up the BVI. This little rock of an island was nestled in the clearest picture postcard perfect surrounding of blue-green water. I made friends quickly and soon developed strong ties with an adopted BVI family and the small family styled church community of which I was a part. My job teaching at the community college paid well. It was a good life. However, there was trouble in paradise. It was during my time living here in the BVI, that I began facing a series of significant existential crises— a quintessential Cherith experience.

After a rocky start, I soon realized that I was not enjoying my job. I felt disconnected from the organizational culture. The workload was also heavy and mentally and professionally exhausting. I wanted out of that situation but not out of the field of higher education. With a master's degree completed, I knew that I needed to earn a doctoral degree to position myself securely in the field. However, no one in my immediate family had navigated college much less a terminal degree. I lacked the social capital—the valuable relational networks to support my academic strivings. As bad as that was, the harsher reality was that I lacked real capital—the money to afford another round of tertiary education. In fact, I was still paying off my master's degree tuition bills. I needed to wait on God for the resources to be able to continue my graduate education.

I was also still single and my biological clock was ticking so loudly that I could barely think of anything else. My desire for marriage and a family were complicated. On one hand, I desperately wanted to be married and to have children. However, thinking about being married to someone for the rest of my life scared me like nothing else. Up to that point in my life, it had become clear to me that I did not possess the discernment that was needed to make a wise and sensible choice of a lifelong mate. I was looking for the wrong things. Big surprise? Well, no not exactly given the circumstances in which I had been raised. What if I got it wrong? What if I repeated the mistakes of my parents?

When it came to having a family of my own, I was plagued by other fears. What if I am not a good mother? How can I even mother when I have not been mothered? These questions and fears played in a constant loop in my mind stymieing my efforts in relationships. As I surveyed my prospects at the time, I realized how I had been sabotaging my own success at every turn. I had trapped myself in a stunted relationship that was going nowhere fast.

Around that same time, my dad, who was still living in Trinidad, had started to experience ill health. He was becoming very forgetful. His most recent visit to the doctor had also indicated some abnormalities with his prostate gland; he was scheduled to undergo a biopsy to test for malignancy. The possibility that the biopsy could reveal the presence of cancerous cells left me feeling anxious. It seemed that even the very shaky one-parent foundation on which my life had been built was crumbling. As the scheduled appointment drew near, I turned to the God who I was growing accustomed to waiting on for answers.

Waiting on God

The weight of these life challenges was heavy on my mind. The limitations of my human capabilities were becoming strikingly evident. So I called out to God—"Help me!" What began as a cry for help, turned into an extended season of intense prayer and pleading with God. I needed help, and I knew He had the answers. Like Hannah in the temple, and like Jacob wrestling with the angel through the night, I was determined that I was not going to stop praying until something happened. And pray I did, crying out to God: "Please help me, God!" I need your guidance and direction!"

During this time, my body developed its own internal alarm clock. I would awake while it was still dark, fall on my knees and pray until the sun came up. I was praying for several things but three things in particular:

My Father's Health—Asking God for a negative cancer biopsy.

Temple University—Asking for a full scholarship to Temple University for doctoral studies.

Husband and Family—Asking God to bring my husband to me and to bless us with children.

I wish I could say that at this time I had a strong and un-wavering faith that God would hear and answer my prayer. I cannot. My faith was more like a quivering, desperate kind of faith--strong one minute and weak the next, but I clutched onto it like a drowning woman clutching at a log. I knew I needed God to show up in my life in a big way.

I decided to do like Gideon and put a fleece out[26]—so I kept a journal. I still have that journal today. As I was writing this book, I looked back to see my scribblings from 2000. Once again I was in awe of what God had done in my life. He did answer my prayers! And yet His answers were not always "Yeses!"

A Father's Health

The biopsy came back positive for cancer. I could not believe it! I was hurt and angry. "What are you doing, God?" I asked. "You have already allowed me to be motherless, are you now going to let me be fatherless too?" Like for real? That news sent me into an emotional tail-spin.

My father was initially diagnosed with prostate cancer and later with Parkinson's disease. Even though a diagnosis of prostate cancer does not signal a death sentence, especially in the context of a developed country with access to quality health care, for those with limited means in the small Caribbean island of Trinidad, it very well might have been. My father was in the latter category. It would require money to get quick and speedy treatment in a private health care facility or relentless advocacy to navigate the public health care system. My father was in his seventies at the time, and he lacked both the money and the supporting cast around him to secure him either, and I was miles away living on another island.

When my prayers for a negative cancer test result were answered with a positive test result, it felt like a terrible blow had been leveled at my fledgling faith. This news was faith crushing. Disillusioned and upset, I thought to myself: "Well, if He has not fulfilled that prayer request the way I hoped, what hope is there that he will work things out for me with my other requests?" I felt like giving up, but I did not. I kept on praying.

A Scholarship

At the urging and sponsorship of a close friend, I applied to the College of Education at Temple University to be in the PhD program in educational psychology. It was a dream. I lacked both the funds and the confidence that I had the academic capabilities to pursue doctoral work. But still, I stepped forward with my shaky faith.

I was accepted!

This acceptance required me to make one of my biggest and boldest prayer requests of God yet. "God," I prayed, "I need to get a scholarship acceptance letter from Temple before I quit my job!" This was critical. To be able to obtain a US student visa, I needed to show that I had enough money in my bank account to support myself as a graduate student. I did not. The other option was to apply for a graduate assistantship scholarship that would cover my tuition and offer a stipend to meet my monthly expenses. That's exactly what I needed! However, these scholarship awards were given only after the first year of continuous and successful enrollment in the program. I could not get the student visa to allow me to enroll in the program without the award letter, but I could only get the award letter after I was enrolled in the program. It was one of those Red Sea moments in my life, where if I was to go forward I needed God to work a miracle.

I traveled to Philadelphia early in 2000, to meet with the dean of the College of Education at Temple University to plead my case. I did not know what I would say. How would I convince him to break the policy for appointment of scholarships and give me a chance? I did not have the words. Yet I distinctly remember sitting in the open office suite of Ritter Hall. I was surrounded by a pool of administrative assistants in the main area where I sat, but behind them were the three closed office doors of the dean and assistant deans. I sat there quietly; my lips were not moving, but I was praying:

> "God I need you to show up in this situation! Please allow me to get the award that I need. You are able to do exceedingly and abundantly above anything I can ask.[27] Please fulfill that promise to me right now."

I was so intent on my prayer that when I heard my name, I wondered if God was speaking to me out loud. But it was one of the administrative assistants. She had called my name as she approached her colleague's desk. "Do you have the award letter for Kathy-Ann Hernandez?" she asked.

"Yes, it's right here," the other said.

"Well, she will need to sign for it. Is she here...?"

I jumped up from my seat: "I am here!"

God had answered, "Yes!"

A Husband and Motherhood

For a period that spanned about a year, I had "come boldly before the throne of God".[28] After reading the book, *God is a Matchmaker*,[29] I was determined to wait on God to make the match for me with my husband. In this book, authors Derek and Ruth Prince remind readers that when God made Adam, he did not have to go out searching for a mate. God brought Eve to Adam, and Adam knew the connection immediately, for he said, "*This is now bone of my bones and flesh of my flesh.*"[30] There was the solution I needed. God is the best matchmaker!

I went to work on my knees. I made a list of ten qualities I was looking for in a mate, and I began committing those to daily prayer: "Please, choose a husband for me, God! I trust you to know what is best for me."

In August of 2000, I arrived in Philadelphia, Pennsylvania from the British Virgin Islands after receiving my award letter for a full scholarship to complete a doctoral degree at Temple University. The first week I was there, I started looking around the city for a church to worship. I called the only friend I knew in Philly at the time to ask his advice. He told me he would call around to see if he could get someone to take me to the nearby church. He did. At ten o'clock the next morning, I came down the three-story flight of stairs in the North Philly brownstone where I lived to meet the young man who had agreed to take me to church that day. When I saw him, God's Spirit said to me, "This is your husband."

After graduating from Temple University in 2004, God opened up another door for me to obtain a tenure track position at a Christian university that same year. In 2006, I married the young man who showed up at my door in 2000—Mark Avery. And God blessed us with two beautiful daughters, one in 2007 and one in 2010.

God had done it again!

Waiting Patterns Ahead

These stories are mile markers in my faith walk with God. This entire chronology: surviving my childhood, migrating to the United States, completing graduate studies at Temple University, and meeting the love of my life happened in a way that only God could orchestrate. These were clear and direct responses to my prayers. They are miraculous victories that testify of God's faithfulness! I cling to them when my faith begins to falter. In spite of all that is wrong in the world, there is a God who is at work in the midst of brokenness championing our cause. He is faithful! That is my testimony. Even so, in spite of what God has done for me in the past, I realize that I am facing new challenges. These answered prayers seem like distant memories.

Perhaps like me you can recollect miraculous answers to past prayers. Yet the obstacles you are facing now are different from anything you have experienced before. They are challenging you in new ways. Maybe, just like me, you have been intentionally trying to seek inspiration by recollecting past victories. However, you still remain less than fully comforted. Those victories were so many years ago. Where is God now? Will He do it again?

∞∞∞

In spite of all that is wrong in the world, there is a God who is at work in the midst of brokenness championing our cause. He is faithful!

Chapter 4. The Brook Experience

Recognizing Brook Experiences

I was nine years old and sitting in my elementary school classroom watching my favorite teacher at work. That was when I decided that I wanted to become a teacher. I remember thinking to myself. "Wow! What a great job!" To be able to live in the world of books and learning and to inspire young minds, what could be a better career choice than teaching? I could not think of one. Right there in that classroom is where the seeds for my teaching career were planted. I was going to be a teacher when I grew up!

From teaching dolls in the back of my father's garage, on to teaching preschool, elementary school, and then college. In spite of some missteps along the way, I finally settled into the world of higher education where I not only got to teach but to practice my other great love, writing. It was a dream come true. Teaching was my calling!

However, around 2015, I began feeling increasingly restless in my profession. It was not so much about a change of direction but a refocusing of my passions and gifts. I became convinced that God was calling me to do something different at this stage in my career. I was not quite sure what that something was, but because of the relationship I have been developing with Him over the years, that voice was strong and clear. And so, spurred on by these Spirit promptings, I began positioning myself to take on senior administrative positions at my own institution and even elsewhere. Although I was still unclear about what that role would be, I was determined to follow where God was leading. I did the networking, served on committees, took on roles and responsibilities that would hone my leadership skills. I sought out mentors and sponsors; I attended leadership conferences and training institutes. I was getting ready to launch out into my new career trajectory.

Then quite serendipitously, I became aware of a job opening for a senior administrative position at a university. I heard God's Spirit saying to me, "This position is for you!" And I was like, "God, are you sure? I don't think I have what it takes for *this* position. God, you know that I don't have the pedigree and the connections. I am not one of *those* people, God! In fact, God I don't really want to move to *that* place. Our family is very settled here. The girls love their schools etc., etc." Like Moses, I continued making excuses.[31]

But still, I could not silence the voice that said: "Yes, I am sure. This job is for you!" So, I read through the job description. What? It described my skill set almost perfectly. In fact, if I had to write a job description to capture the full range of my leadership experiences up to that point, that is what I would have written. But still less than fully convinced, I decided to apply. All the while, I was thinking to myself, "They are not going to pick you."

Well, to my surprise, but certainly not to God's, I made it to the short list of ten. Then I made it to the shortlist of five, and then the short shortlist of two. I did the job talks, and I had a one-on-one conversation with the president of the university. It was clear that I was more than qualified for the position. Hesitant though we were, Mark and I committed the entire process to God's will. I said, "God if you keep opening the doors, I am just going to keep walking through." So I kept on walking in faith. Though my confidence was shaky, my faith in God was resolute —God was calling me and taking me through this process for a reason.

And then, the door shut!

The door shut in my face! Yes, it did!

Just as I was about to pull the handle and walk through, the door slammed shut!

I did not get the job.

That was bad enough, but shortly thereafter other doors began closing as well. The networks I had been cultivating so diligently among leaders at my own institution and other higher institutional contexts also began to fray one by one. People moved on or were fired, and leadership changed hands. The brook had dried up, and now I found myself with a call on my life but hidden beside a dried-up brook!

Understanding Brook Experiences

At the time this happened, I was confused and angry. In fact, on many mornings during this period, I remember returning from my regular morning walk and launching into a long rant to my husband, Mark. "What was that all about?" I asked. "You know, I was not even looking for that job. Why did God take me on that journey, only to leave me locked out? I just don't get it?"

Neither one of us had been excited about what that job offer would have meant for our lives. Among many other cons, the position would also involve a cut in salary. I kid you not! But God had spoken and whether we understood His reasoning or not, we had desired to obey. So why had he sent me on that failing mission and now put in hiding for almost three years and counting? Why?

At the core, brook experiences are waiting moments in our relationship with God when we often feel most alone and uncertain about what's next for us. A brook experience puts us in a position of vulnerability—it is a place where we have been confronted with some personal, social or professional life challenge or injustice for which we must rely on God to successfully navigate. Brook experiences require us to wait on God when we lack clarity about next steps, and even when we don't understand what has happened or why.

Having been in this cycle many times, let me share with you some observations I have made about brook experiences.

Opportunities to Mend a Broken Relationship

Brook experiences are a defining characteristic of living in a sin infested world. In Eden, Adam enjoyed unhindered communication with God. Sin changed all that. There was now a break in the relationship between the created and the Creator. As a result of sin, the relational ties between us and God need repairing. From a very practical level, and in keeping with the focus of this book, the Christian experience is about taking steps that are necessary for us to reconnect with our Maker. That involves a retraining of our mind and our heart—our spiritual ears to hear God's voice and follow where He leads us.

In the book *Whisper*, Mark Batterson suggests that God has six languages that He uses to communicate with us: scripture, people, pain, desires, doors, and dreams.[32] According to Batterson, whichever language God uses, He chooses to speak to us in a "whisper." A whispering voice is indicative of intimacy—of closeness. We need to get very close to someone to be able to hear what is being said in a whisper.[33] The place in which we are often best positioned to hear God's whispering voice in a too distracted world, is when we find ourselves sitting beside our brook, waiting on Him.

A constant challenge for each of us in our growing maturity as a believer is to learn how to navigate the daily hurdles that constantly wedge their way into our developing relationship with God. These challenges can be seemingly as innocuous as an overly busy schedule where we are so busy that we squeeze out quality time to spend with God. But at other times the challenge we face may be the result of more deeply rooted issues. For example, because of an imperfect relational connection with God in a sin infected world, we often desire things that are outside of God's will for our life and are ultimately not in our best interest.[34] Waiting on God then becomes a process for us to bring our will into alignment with His.

Additionally, as part of the larger cosmic struggle in which we exist as believers, brook experiences are often attack strategies that the Enemy uses in his attempt to block the blessings God has in store for us. The experience of Daniel is particularly compelling.[35] In Daniel chapter 10, we are told that on the first day that Daniel knelt down to pray, God dispatched an angel in answer to Daniel's prayer, but it was not until twenty-one days later that the angel arrived. Why? The angel reports that a spiritual being tried to block the way: *the spirit prince of the kingdom of Persia blocked my way.*"[36] But God sent help so that the angel could finally get to Daniel in response to his prayers.

Whatever the reasons are for why we might be experiencing delays, our positioning by the brook at a particular time in our Christian experience is a place where we have an opportunity to do the work that is necessary to mitigate the separating effects of sin on our relationship with God.

Answers to our Prayers

Brook experiences often come in answer to our prayers. We may pray for God to move in our lives in a specific way. However, when He does answer, it is not exactly what we prayed for. We may not even recognize then that our current waiting challenge is in fact an answer to our prayers because it involves struggle. It involves pain. But wait! Aren't answered prayers supposed to be moments of celebration? No! Not always.

Here is a personal example. After I prayed for a husband and Mark came into my life, I had no doubt that God brought him to be my husband. How did I know? Well, I kept a prayer journal in which I had written down ten qualities I wanted in a mate. Mark matched eight of those qualities. Not exactly 100%, but of the ten items, the ones he matched were the most important. Second, the moment I met him, God's Spirit gave me the calm assurance that this was my future mate.

Even so, my dating experience with Mark was simultaneously one of most wonderful and one of most infuriatingly difficult dating experiences of my life. Let's just say we had "issues to work out!" Among other issues was the work needed for us to navigate through our cultural differences and find a soft place for our love to land. There were tense moments, challenging moments, when we both wanted to walk away from the promise of a happily ever after ending.

But if God had brought Mark to me, why was it so hard? Well, because brook experiences as a result of answered prayer are not without struggle. Even in the space of answered prayers we might experience pain. God often leads us through painful experiences, through the broken places of our lives for a divine purpose that will be revealed if we are able to navigate the wait successfully.

I did experience moments of questioning God about why he was allowing me/us to go through this challenging dating experience. However, whenever these doubts surfaced, I was able to center myself in the assurance that if God had brought us to this spot, He was at work behind it all. I could trust Him!

Now when Mark and I reflect on those experiences, we are convinced that in the process of doing the hard work to get over these teething issues, we were also developing a deeper appreciation for each other and the relationship we now share that is the foundation of our marriage. We are also convinced that we are better parents because of the wait—more patient, more appreciative of the joys and pains of parenting, and in a better position financially to take care of our children and our family.

As our relationship with God develops, God often brings us to answered prayers that are brook experiences—they involve struggle. We can come to recognize them because of the relationship we are developing with Him. We learn to hear his voice, and we are confident of His will in our lives because it conforms to what he has said in His word—the Bible. Even though these experiences may be painful, we continue to trust

God because we are confident that He has a plan for us through the experience.

Transformation of our Missteps

Brook experiences can also come into our lives because of our own actions—wrong choices that we make. While we wait for our prayers to be answered or are even in the midst of the answer, we may get tired of waiting. We may get tired because the experience is painful or the wait is long. At times, we may decide that it is best to take matters into our own hands. Instead of waiting on God, we orchestrate circumstances to create the outcome for which we hope. Unfortunately, in attempting to play the role of God in our own lives, we often end up creating a more difficult path to the outcome that God has promised us. The amazing thing is that even when we act contrary to His will, God still chooses to find us and take our mess ups and our mistakes and refashion them into pivotal transforming moments in our relationship with Him. However, there is a prerequisite for this transformative experience—earnest repentance.

We can see God's intervention and transforming power in the life experience of King David. David committed sin after sin, first taking another man's wife, then scheming for the death of her husband so he could marry her. If ever there was a mess up —David committed it big time! However, when God confronts David with his sin through the prophet Nathan, David confesses his sins; he is sorry about what he has done. He asks God to forgive him. He pleads with God to create his heart anew so that he would not do it again.[37] David's repentance is one of the most beautiful repentances that is penned in the Bible. When our own actions lead us to brook experiences, we, like the psalmist David, must recognize our errors, confess them to God and commit to turning away from them.

Other times though, mistakes are not of our choosing but because of the brokenness of this world. There will be many things that happen to us in life that we will not understand. Things that happen to us because we live in a world where everything has been broken by sin. In reflecting on some of the difficult moments in my life, I don't understand why my mother abandoned me. I don't understand why my father got prostate cancer. And yet, when I think back on these and other difficult life experiences, I recognize that God was transforming these missteps into blessings. These experiences were the seeds that have produced in me a unique perspective borne out of the depth of these life challenges. I can now say like Joseph said to his brothers: *"You planned evil against me but God used those same plans for my good."*[38]

Each of us will face problems along our life journey. Some of these problems will be because of our own choices, while others will happen to us because of the evil that is in the world. However, we serve a God who still chooses to transform problems and missteps into blessings.

One-on-One Encounters with God

Brook experiences are one-on-one encounters with God. We might be going through a life crisis surrounded by a supportive circle of loved ones—our spouse, parents, friends, and our children. Navigating our brook experiences might involve confrontation or collaboration with others to achieve the outcome for which we hope, or perhaps confessions about wrongs done against others. We may choose to share the details of the experience with those who are close to us, or we may even seek advice from other spiritual guides. However, none of these individuals is equipped to lead us through our brook experience. At best, they can offer us only limited guidance for the journey ahead. Ultimately, brook experiences are about a personal encounter between each of us and God.

Over the course of my married life, I have faced many personal challenges, moments where God seemed distant and even silent. During many of those times, I found comfort in talking to

Mark, and he has always listened. However, as I worked my way through these difficulties, the most important conversations that I needed to have did not involve Mark at all.

On many mornings, I would slip out of bed quietly so as not to wake him. I would walk past the girls' bedrooms as they slept, and then make my way to my quiet praying spot. This is where I would pour my heart out to God sometimes in anguished groans with tears streaming down my cheeks, and I would share with Him my innermost thoughts. Even if Mark were physically present on those mornings, even if he got up and decided to join me in prayer and was kneeling right beside me, he could not enter into this interaction between God and me. It is this kind of encounter with God that marks the brook experience as custom designed for each individual.

The brook presents a respite, a time apart for us to have that deep one-on-one encounter with God. It is an opportunity for us to come to know and experience God personally because our destiny is wrapped up in cultivating a deeper level of intimacy with Him.

Spot Between the "No Longer" but "Not Yet"

Brook experiences are characterized by a middle of the road positioning. We sense that God is calling us to a different experience and that our present positioning is no longer the place for us to be. However, we do not know exactly what He is calling us to do next, or He has not yet opened the door to fulfill what He has promised for our lives. This liminal space can make us quite dissatisfied with our current state of affairs. We can experience feelings of restlessness and frustration as we wait on God to open up a new door for us to walk through. We hear God whispering to us about the future plans He has in store for us, and just as we begin to get excited, He tells us to "Stay here. Don't move." How frustrating!

This is a familiar pattern in the experiences of many Bible characters. For example, Abraham was promised at the age of

45

seventy-five that he would be the father of many nations. However, it would take another twenty-five years till the birth of the promised son Isaac. Then, as I explore later in this book, there are the experiences of Hannah, Joseph, David, Jacob, and many others. All these individuals waited in the answer of a call on their life which was still to be realized. I imagine that while they waited on God they experienced moments of doubt and dissatisfaction. Maybe they wondered how much longer they would have to wait for God to do what He had promised.

The brook experience is characterized by this growing discomfort with our current situation but waiting on God to clear the path for us to advance forward in the direction of His calling on our life.

Faithful Provisions of God

God continues to provide for us as we wait beside the brook. The prophet Elijah experienced this first hand. There was a famine in the land, but God sent ravens to provide bread and meat for Elijah and cool water for him to drink from the brook.[39] Even when the brook dries up, God continues to provide. He sends Elijah to the widow of Zarephath. It is here that God intervenes again in a miraculous way and turns *"a handful of flour left in the jar and a little cooking oil"*[40] into a never-ending supply. The widow is able to feed Elijah, herself and her son through the remaining years of the famine. These two experiences have one common element —the faithful provisions of God. This is what the psalmist observes when he reflects on his life: *"I was young and now I am old, yet I have never seen the righteous forsaken or their children begging bread."*[41]

God takes care of his children even while they wait, oftentimes in difficult life situations. In prison, the Apostle Paul had continued visits from his young friend Timothy, and he asks Timothy to bring him some of his comforting possessions: *"When you come, be sure to bring the coat I left with Carpus at Troas. Also bring my books, and especially my papers."*[42]

When we come to our brook experiences whether He brings us to it, or transforms our mess ups into brook experiences, a loving God continues to provide for us as we wait on Him. He gives us what we need. We may not have everything that we want. It may represent a fall from our accustomed station in life. We may lack the luxuries to which we have grown accustomed, but we have the confident assurance that God's provisions will be enough.

Positions of Obscurity

A brook experience is often a position of obscurity. It is a place of isolation that God brings us to when He is about to do something great in our lives. Even Jesus himself, went through these moments of isolation in preparation for ministry. For example, just before Jesus began his ministry on earth, we are told, *"Then Jesus was led by the Spirit into the wilderness to be tempted by the devil."*[43] Jesus stayed there for 40 days and 40 nights.

Then on the night before He was crucified, we see Jesus alone again in the Garden of Gethsemane.[44] His disciples are asleep, but Jesus is by Himself in the waiting zone—facing the greatest test of His earthly ministry—He pleads with his father to strengthen Him for what is about to happen next.

There are many more examples that we can draw from in the Bible. Moses was stuck away in Midian for 40 years.[45] According to Bible historians, Daniel was exiled in Babylon; it is estimated for about seventy years. Then there is the Apostle Paul, struck down on the road to Damascus before his name was changed from Saul. Paul does not immediately go to Jerusalem. Instead he flees to Damascus where he is taken to the house of Judas for a few days before his sight is returned to him through God's messenger Ananias.[46] There, under threat of his life, he hurriedly goes to Arabia. Paul spends three years here in relative obscurity. We are not given any details about how he spent his time here before he returns to Jerusalem to launch into full ministry. However, as Paul later writes to the Galatians, the gospel he ends up preaching was taught to him "*by the revelation of Jesus Christ himself.*"[47] We can infer that this kind of revelation came to the apostle after spending much time deepening his connection with God. These three men, Moses, Daniel and Paul, as well as many others, all experienced extended periods of "hiding" in preparation for ministry.

Brook experiences are often "hiding" moments that can test our faith. In this space, we might begin to question God's methods and or the reason for His delay. We might even begin to lose hope that the calling on our lives will ever be realized. However, the brook is a critical point in our journey where we have an opportunity to lean deeper into our relationship with God in preparation for where He is taking us next.

Brook Experiences and the Christian Journey

Brook experiences come to all at some time and often multiple times during our life journey. As I have talked with many others in the faith and outside the faith, I have recognized this common positioning. I have talked to women waiting to get married, waiting to have children, hoping to pursue higher education, praying for healing for themselves or others, praying for their children to return to God, praying for financial resources, praying for emotional healing, and even dealing with betrayal by those they trusted. I have talked to men and women in line for job promotions who continue to be ignored or marginalized, not because they lack qualifications or competence, but because the system is unjust and stacked against them. I have also met others who were simply asking God to clarify next steps in trying to figure out their life work.

My own experiences and that of so many other Bible characters like Elijah illustrate that at one time and/or multiple times we will occupy this waiting space—"the brook". Whenever these waiting moments come, we can be confident that God will continue to provide for us during these challenging times. We also have the full assurance that God is able to transform our missteps and mess ups into looking up moments. The brook becomes a resting spot. It is a place where we can experience a renewed commitment to God and preparation for what lies ahead.

It is in these waiting spaces that we can find the path to more intimate one-on-one encounters with God, but we must do the work that is necessary for us to wait patiently on Him.

∞∞∞

A brook experience puts us in a position of vulnerability —it is a place where we have been confronted with some personal, social or professional life challenge or injustice for which we must rely on God to successfully navigate. Brook experiences require us to wait on God when we lack clarity about next steps, and even when we don't understand what has happened or why.

Chapter 5. Waiting Patiently

The Posture of Waiting

As the bus made its way to this "where-in-the-world-are-we-going" corner spot of Washington State, the organizers of the Leadership Institute assured us that the retreat center where we were headed was worth the effort. "The food is great!" "The grounds are beautiful!" Under my breath I muttered, "Well, I will just wait and see about that!" For one thing, this was Father's Day weekend, and I was going to be away from my family. For another thing, I was already thinking of the almost twelve-hour wait at the airport that I would have to endure on my flight back to Philly the following week. However, the next words from the lead organizer's mouth made me turn away from the window and pay attention: "This Christian retreat center is one of those *thin places* on earth."

Hmmmh? Thin places? I had not heard this expression before. I needed to find out more, so I did a quick Internet search on my phone. I learned that the term "thin places" might have originated among the Irish, but it is most often connected to the Celtics. Thin places represented doorways to other spiritual worlds. These spaces were often indicated on physical objects like stones with large spirals carved onto the surface. It was believed that these thin spaces held some mystical or spiritual power—in this location deep spiritual contemplation was possible.

What an intriguing concept! Though not in alignment with my own faith tradition, I find the concept of thin places a useful metaphor for how brook experiences often situate us in a space where we can interact with God in more meaningful ways.

After spending a few days at the retreat center, I did experience God in a deeper way for several reasons. First, we did our best to disconnect from the usual distractions of everyday life. We had no television sets in our rooms, and taking the wise advice from the retreat organizers, we chose to turn our phone's off during the all-day sessions. We made time for early morning walks around the natural grounds and midafternoon hikes through the woods. I began those days in the prayer garden asking God, "What would you have me do today?" I waited on God in this place.

When we choose to wait patiently on God, we are opening up a soul-window to heaven that provides us with an up-close view of God and a thin place for Him to connect with us. It is only through the process of waiting patiently on Him, that we can begin the process of adopting new paradigms that equip us to fully occupy the thin space of the brook experience.

In the book *The Seven Habits of Highly Effective People*, Stephen Covey defines a paradigm shift as a shift in our way of seeing things. We experience an "Aha!" moment. Covey explains that "paradigm shifts move us from one way of seeing the world to another. And these shifts create powerful change."[48]

There are four paradigm shifts that are necessary for us to navigate the brook experience successfully.

Ending or Beginning?

Behold, I will do a new thing; now it shall spring forth; shall ye not know it? I will even make a way in the wilderness, and rivers in the desert.[49]

Stop for a moment and ask yourself: "Is the spot where I currently find myself the ending of a thing or the beginning of something even better?" Are you waiting by the brook, or are you beginning to climb the mountain? The answer is that it all depends.

As I think back about my experience with that now infamous job application process, I will admit that when I received the email that I had not gotten the job, I was crushed. It did seem like the ending of an aspiration and dream. However, as I spent more time in that space, I slowly began to reframe how I was thinking about that experience. Yes, it was the end of the line for my hopes for *that* job at this time. But it could also mark the beginning of other hopes.

After Mark and I had reflected on the experience for a bit, one day he said to me wisely, "Kathy, what if it was not about the job at all? What if this experience was about teaching you to enlarge the vision that you have for your life?" Wow! That question gave me a moment of pause. Certainly, before this experience, I had locked myself into a confining script of "college professor." What if God had allowed me to come to this ending, so I could begin to embrace that larger vision for my life?

Each brook experience is different, and though the circumstance of your closed door may be contextually different from mine, the same characteristics apply as discussed in chapter 4. How we experience this waiting period depends on how we choose to label it. For believers, the labeling is actually quite simple. God has already given the label; it is a new thing![50] It is a beginning! If we can make this paradigm shift in our thinking, we will see brook experiences for what they are—gifted time to prepare us for the Mount Carmel experiences that are coming. A brook experience can mark the end of a dream or the birthplace of new aspirations.

Punishment or Preparation?

No discipline seems pleasant at the time, but painful. Later on, however, it produces a harvest of righteousness and peace for those who have been trained by it.[51]

Is your brook experience punishment or preparation? Your

location may not change, but your mind can transport you to a different setting altogether. Richard Lovelace, in the well-known poem "To Althea, from Prison," writes about the freedom we can experience even in the harshest of circumstance:

> Stone Walls do not a Prison make,
> Nor Iron bars a Cage;
> Minds innocent and quiet take
> That for an Hermitage.
> If I have freedom in my Love,
> And in my soul am free,
> Angels alone that soar above,
> Enjoy such Liberty.[52]

As we go through brook experiences, our ability to get the most out of these experiences is reflective of the perspective we bring to them. If we come to view this season of our life as punishment, we will continue to suffer through it. We will be at risk of squandering the time we have been given, lamenting the challenges and difficulties of our current situation, feeling sorry for ourselves and not being able to focus on the lessons. That would be tragic.

The Bible illustrates for us with story after story, how for those individuals who God was able to use mightily, He allowed them to go through a season of waiting. We need no better example than that of God's own son, Jesus. For the first thirty years of His life, not much is recorded about Him in any of the four Gospels. Do you wonder what Jesus might have been thinking, feeling or doing during this time? From the very beginning, He knew the call that His Father had on His life, and yet He had to wait. Did He grumble? Was He suffering through this time as a form of punishment, or was He making the best use of the time to prepare Himself for His ministry.

I suggest that it was the latter. Jesus used this season of waiting as preparation for the work that He was called to do. How do I know? Well, here is one telling example. At the age of twelve, the scriptures record that He remained in the Temple with the elders, long after His parents, Mary and Joseph had left Jerusalem. When they came back to find Him, we are told, *After three days they found him in the temple courts, sitting among the teachers, listening to them and asking them questions. Everyone who heard him was amazed at his understanding and his answers.*[53]

Later, we see Him at the start of His public ministry. He is baptized by John the Baptist and immediately heads into the wilderness. There He is able to stand up to the temptations of the Devil and be victorious because He has been preparing for this very confrontation.[54]

The early period of Jesus' life and His time in the wilderness were times of preparation for three years of effective and compassionate ministry. To be successful in ministry, He needed to take advantage of this gift of time in the early years.

Our dark moments rightly used and understood can prepare us for ministry and service in a way that seasons of ease and abundance cannot! A brook experience can be our breaking point, or it can be our making point.

Resignation or Expectation?

Not that I speak in respect of want: for I have learned, in whatsoever state I am, therewith to be content.[55]

While we wait by the brook, we must resist the temptation to resign ourselves to our fate here. The brook is not meant to be a permanent resting spot; it is a place of transition. However, navigating the delicate balance between acceptance of where we are positioned in our Christian journey and hope for the future can be a bit tricky. In this position, we are called to balance the contradicting emotions of contentment and discontentment. Learning to put our trust and confidence in God even when we go through valley experiences is the sign of a maturing faith which God requires of us. At the same time, God's plans for us are *"exceedingly abundantly above all that we ask or think."*[56] Hence, there is a temptation for Elijah at the brook to be content with this "just enough" experience—to be satisfied with bread and water from the ravens; to be satisfied with a little flour and oil from the widow of Zarephath—to be content with a mere earthly existence, when God has plans to lift him off the earthly plain of existence and take him up in a chariot of fire! This is what the Lord says: *"'I know the plans I have for you,' declares the LORD, 'plans to prosper you and not to harm you, plans to give you hope and a future.'"*[57]

But there is also a subtler reason for why we may become satisfied with the brook experience. We may settle here because we have given in to despair. In this spot, we may let go of the larger vision for our life and settle for a *drying brook* life experience —we choose to close the door off on expectations for the future not because we are content with our current lot, but because we have given up hope that God will deliver on His promises to us. Instead of being a place of new beginnings, we choose to make the brook the place of a premature ending.

However, Cherith is not a place for us to be satisfied with less than what God has in store for us, nor is it a place for us to set up permanent residence because we have lost hope or are too afraid to move on to the next phase of the journey. During our brook experience, we must simultaneously rest contently in God's benevolent provisions for the present, while being discontent with our current positioning for mission and calling. It is in this space of righteous discontentment that we are best able to lay hold of and claim the promise God has for our life. We cannot get too comfortable here as some others have done.

I have been struck by the experience of Abraham's father, Terah. We read in Genesis 11[58] that Terah takes his family and sets out from Ur of the Chaldeans for the promised land of Canaan. However, when he gets to the village of Haran, he sets up camp there. This is where he dies. Yet God's plan for His children has been that they would inherit the promised land of Canaan. After Terah's death, it falls on Abraham to take up the charge again to get to Canaan.

Unlike what happened to Terah, our brook experiences must not lure us into a passive acceptance of our current circumstances. God has bigger plans for us—plans that are about abundance and fulfilling His will for our lives. While we wait by the brook, we must adopt and live in the space of great expectations. A brook experience can mark our burial ground or it can become the best lookout spot for us to view the road ahead.

Dependence or Collaboration?

I can do all things through Christ who strengthens me.[59]

Is our brook experience about helpless dependence or an invitation to a collaborative partnership with God? I suggest that it is the latter. Inasmuch as God wants us to depend on Him as we wait, we make a serious mistake if we think waiting means sitting by idly twiddling our thumbs. God makes provisions for the answer to our prayers, but he invites us to work with Him towards the solution.

What do I mean by that? Well, God's answers to prayers often invite us to be co-workers in the working it out process. Now I want to be clear about this; God does not need us to work with Him to make His will come to pass. However, the more I study His word, I am struck by the many instances in scripture where we see an invitation extended to individuals to be part of the solution to a problem for which God does not really need any help.

In Eden, God invites Adam to be part of the creative process by taking care of the garden and naming the animals.[60] God invites Jacob in his long sojourn with his abusive and manipulative uncle Laban to follow very strict instructions to ensure that the offspring of animals would turn out striped, spotted, or speckled.[61] In His first miracle, Jesus asks the servants at the wedding in Cana to fill the vessels with water.[62] He tells the blind man to walk to the pool and wash the mud off his eyes so that he can see.[63] Then we see God sending Elijah to a widow with a little oil and flour where the widow must turn the flour into dough to make bread before the miracle of a never ending supply can take place.[64] Interesting, isn't it? God delights in having us unite the gifts He has given us in support of the calling He has for our lives. In this way we bring honor to Him through our calling.

In the book *Soar*,[65] the renowned preacher, author and entrepreneur T.D. Jakes explains it this way. God never built a chair or made a table for us even though He knew that these would be useful items for us in life. Instead, he provided us with trees. Similarly, God did not make paper for us or dig wells, yet he provided the natural resources and gave us the mental capacity to use what He has given for our benefit and good. Our role is to use our creativity, use the gifts He has given, apply the wisdom set forth in His word united with the wisdom passed on to us from others, and listen to the promptings of the Holy Spirit to move from provisions to solutions.

It is a misconception to think that while we are "waiting by the brook" this is a time when God will do it all for us. Instead, viewed properly, this is the season where God invites us into an intimate collaboration with him to accomplish His purpose in our life. However, without the right mindset, we can miss the invitation altogether. Brook experiences can be periods of dormancy or periods of intentional activity where we seek to do all that we can to bring our will into alignment with God's purpose for our life.

Seven Action Steps in Waiting

Brook experiences are not reserved for Christians alone. In His great love for us, God allows moments of intervention and rest for us to recalibrate our life journey. A brook experience is a rescuing spot; it is a place where we are ideally situated to look up.

However, this is also a perplexing spot. It is a place of seeming contradictions. It is here that we are challenged to accept that what we see is not what is really before us. This ability to see what cannot be seen is the purest definition of faith: "*Now faith is confidence in what we hope for and assurance about what we do not see.*"[66] We are challenged when we might be at our lowest point emotionally to refocus the lens and see that where we are positioned is not an ending but the beginning of a mountain top ascension; it is not a place of punishment but of preparation for more effective service. It is not a place of resignation—not our final destination but a resting spot on the way to a higher purpose and calling. Finally, it is not a place that calls us to helpless acceptance of our fate. It is a gracious invitation by the Creator to involve us, His creation, in the exciting process of mission fulfillment.

If we look carefully at the lives of several Bible characters, we will be able to trace seven actions that were necessary for them, like us, to successfully navigate brook experiences and achieve these paradigm shifts in thinking. The steps are as follows:

Step 1. **Grieving the Loss**
Step 2. **Wrestling with God**
Step 3. **Pivoting to Praise**
Step 4. **Developing in Darkness**
Step 5. **Encouraging Ourselves in God,**
Step 6. **Persisting in the Face of Challenges**
Step 7. **Profiting from the Pain**

Seven Action Steps in Waiting

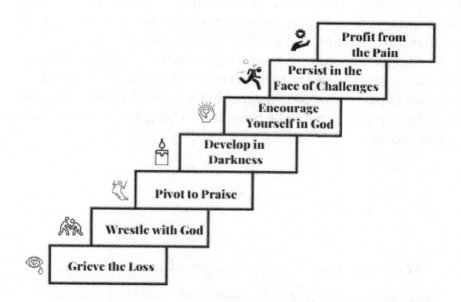

These actions are not neatly linear or necessarily chrono-logical. They are dynamic, overlapping, and iterative. We often go in and out of various action steps as we wait on God. The critical characteristic of each step is that it requires action on our part. When we choose to take intentional action in relating to God, we are well positioned to navigate the wait successfully. And it is in this position that we are able to receive the gifts that God eagerly wants to give us—deeper intimacy with Him, spir-itual transformation, and a call to meaningful service.

In the next section, I draw on personal experience and the lives of selected Bible characters to illustrate each of these steps in turn. I explain how by engaging in these actions, we can posi-tion ourselves to benefit the most from this gift of time waiting by the brook.

When we choose to wait patiently on God, we are open-ing up a soul-window to heaven that provides us with an up-close view of God and a thin place for Him to con-nect with us.

Part 3

Chapter 6. Step 1: Grieve the Loss

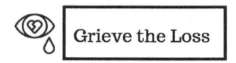 Grieve the Loss

About Mom

If I did not know a mother's love through birth, I came to experience it through marriage. When Mark and I married, I found a mother. "Mom" is the word that best captures her—all hugs and kisses, presents and perfume, laughter and good times, birthday cakes and apple cobblers, holidays and cheer, and grandchildren and treats. On the very first day that Mark and I met, he took me to church and brought me to sit with the rest of his family. From where I sat, about three seats down from her, I could feel the warmth of her spirit embracing me. She smiled at me warmly. Many years later, Mark would tell me that in a quiet moment, she had pulled him over and whispered in his ear, "I like her!"

Mom anticipated the moves she needed to make in the life of this motherless daughter that she inherited. She stepped in on cue for all the big mother-daughter life moments. It was mom who took me to bridal store after bridal store, in search of that just right dress. I remember well the moment when we found THE dress. As I came out of the dressing room, our eyes locked in a watery embrace compelling our arms to soon follow; we hugged each other tightly and cried openly.

But wait, there is more! When my first daughter was born, I remember well the anxieties and uncertainties that welled up within me. Could I do this? What was this that I had to do? How could I be a good mother when I had not been mothered? So many fears! But "Mom" had it covered. When Mark and I arrived home from the hospital that afternoon in late October, I could see her bent frame through the kitchen window; she was busy at work. When we walked into the house, the aroma of home cooking enveloped us, and her arms encircled me. She fussed over me, fussed over the baby, fussed over her chocolate cake —fuss, fuss, fuss—and I..., shucks, I thoroughly enjoyed it. The truth is, I needed it! Mom stayed with us for several days helping me adjust to my new role. Ah, what a gift!

And so, it was in April of 2013 that I had an idea that I wanted to host a Mother's Day brunch for mom to show her just how much we valued her and all that she was to us. When I broached the idea to Mark, who is totally a "mama's boy," I could tell that he was touched. He said simply, "Perhaps, flesh and blood has not revealed this to you!" [67] Then he added, "But that will mean giving up your Mother's Day. Don't you mind?" I did not mind. Mom deserved it.

So being what some of my friends have called "A Black Martha Stewart Wanna-Be," I was off to the races in creating a memorable event (Don't judge me, okay!). I bought some fabric, dusted off my sewing machine and sewed an apron for Mom. Then I searched online for the perfect cupcake motifs to glue on it representing her children and grandchildren. We planned a delicious over-the-top brunch with some of her favorites— homemade, of course. The four siblings and their spouses and her grandchildren got together at our house, and we showered her with gifts and tributes of love. We were all dressed in jeans with white tops, and we fiddled and fussed outside the house against the background of white and pink azaleas, taking way too long to get the perfect family photo.

That day we told her just how much she meant to us. I told her how much I loved her, and how I appreciated the way that she was loving me. Her eyes brimmed with a kind of tearful joy. Our outpouring of love had taken her by surprise, and she said: "Wow! I can't believe you kids did all of this for me." And then she wondered out loud for a moment: "Do you think I will be around for the next Mother's Day?" We shushed away any such thoughts from her head; we laughed away the very suggestion. What an awesome time we had that day!

We had no idea that it would be the last Mother's Day that she would spend with us.

Dealing with Loss

In October of 2013, my family and I were hurting. "Mom" had taken ill suddenly. Within the space of a few days, we saw her deteriorate rapidly without a clear diagnosis in sight. What started out as a pain in her abdomen became lost in "doctor speak" and tests, and hospital visits, and specialists and breathing machines until she did not look anything like the woman we loved. Then one night, in mid-November, the siblings and spouses gathered in a cramped hospital room to say our last goodbyes.

The following year, the grief from Mom's passing was still fresh in my mind, so I recognized this now familiar presence in the lives of a few of the students I teach. These are graduate students who lead very busy lives as spouses, parents, teachers/professionals trying to manage it all in the pursuit of higher education. There they were juggling it all in the middle of a busy and taxing semester. Still even with so many balls in the air, the unexpected happened and every ball threatened to come crashing down on them. This particular semester was an especially trying one for three students in my class—an only child and single parent taking care of her own family and making endless trips to the hospital as she dealt with the debilitating health of her own mother; a young man whose heart was breaking as he waited for news about the survival of his first child who would eventually die before making it out of the hospital;

and a mother of two planning funeral services for her last living parent—her mom. I felt my heart breaking for them like it did for our family on November 13, 2013—the night "Mom" passed away.

Perhaps, there is no grief that is as palpable as the grief of losing a loved one. However, death is not the only thing that can cause us to grieve. Grief can be broadly defined as mental suffering or distress in response to a real or perceived loss. These losses can include death of another person, or even loss of one's possessions, job, status, or ideals. Grief then can come to us at different times in our lives as we experience personal loss.

Reflecting on my childhood experiences of loss, I realize that for much of my early years prior to my mother's arrival at our home on that fateful day, I had been waiting in hopeful expectation. Those hopes were dashed at that visit. Whereas the years prior to her visit had been marked by hopeful expectation, the years after were tinged with grief and dealing with the loss of my mother. A few years after that visit, I remember sitting at my desk in my elementary school classroom. It was close to Mother's Day and the teacher had us all to create a card for our mother telling her how special she was in our lives. I looked at the blank piece of paper on my desk. I had nothing to write— there were no moments to recollect when my mother had held me, put a band-aid on my knee, read to me, or hugged me. I sat there for a minute or so, while the tears welled up in my eyes, and then they rolled down my cheek. I buried my head in my desk, and I cried.

I grieved for many years after that—as a teenager, and later as a young adult. But still, I did not know how to process that grief. I did not know how to deal with the reality of waiting in vain for a hope to be realized that just wasn't ever going to happen.

Processing Grief

We are not given many details about the inner life of some of the major Bible characters, but certainly they were like us all, fallible human beings. In the case of Elijah, I imagine that in his time by the brook, there was much for him to grieve about. Elijah had prayed for the drought, with little thought about his own safety, but rather as a drastic move so that the children of Israel could return to the one true God. But now that his prayers had been answered, did he continue to grieve Israel's apostasy as he sat beside the brook? Did he regret that it had to come to this —a season of drought and famine? All around him, the people of God were suffering. Some individuals would most likely die. How personally would these deaths touch him? At a time in his own life, when he could have been sharing the message throughout the camp, he has entered into this season of obscurity and isolation. Was he lonely? Was he discouraged? Why had God left him in this state of uncertainty about his next assignment? We don't know the answers to these questions, but I imagine that Elijah experienced various emotions as he sat beside the brook.

In 1969, Swiss-American psychiatrist, Elisabeth Kübler-Ross, identified stages of grief in her book *Death and Dying*.[68] Though these stages were associated with death and or terminal illness, they also apply for dealing with other losses in our lives. The five stages of grief are identified as follows:

> **Denial**: We deny that this can be happening to us.
>
> **Anger:** We question why it happened and/or who is to blame.
>
> **Bargaining**: We often bargain with God, to make it not happen or go away, and I will...
>
> **Depression:** We sink into depression thinking, "I can't bear this; I'm too sad to do anything.
>
> **Acceptance:** We come to acknowledge that it has

happened, and we cannot change it.

This model is very useful in showing the range of emotions that can accompany grief, but it is just a framework. We may or may not go through these stages in sequence. Some have suggested that grief is far too personal to be neatly wrapped up in a stage model. Rather, we need to understand grief as a process that reflects the experience of bereaved persons, "their thoughts and feelings" that are unique to every individual.[69] Whether grief is best described through this neat model or as unique experiences is not really the important thing. What is important is that we acknowledge that to be able to deal with losses in our lives and get past them, we must go *through* the process of grieving.

Jesus and Grief

My own experience in dealing with losses in my life as a Christian, and also observing how we sometimes comfort those going through loss, is that too often we do a lousy job of comforting people. We do not give them enough time to grieve. It is almost as if we expect that faith in God should inoculate us/them from grieving. After all, we are told in Scripture to *"rejoice at all times."*[70] The unspoken expectation is that we should not dwell too long in the state of grief. Rather, it would seem like we are almost expected to move in one giant leap from loss to joyful acceptance. This is not a healthy response to loss, and it is not based on scriptural evidence!

When Jesus is confronted with the grief of others, He does not tell them to "Just, cheer up!" or that *"all things work together for the good."*[71] No! Instead, He often chooses to share in the grief of those who are hurting, and He acts to relieve their suffering. We see Jesus traveling to Bethany to comfort two grieving sisters;[72] We see Him offering fishing advice and then making breakfast for a boat full of weary fishermen.[73] There He is on bended knee making mud with His own saliva and putting it on the eyes of a blind man.[74] Can you see Him holding the hands of a little girl as her parents grieve outside and saying the life-giving words: *"Little girl, I say to you, get up!"*[75]?

What is more, Jesus is described by the prophet Isaiah as a man who knew what it was to grieve. Isaiah writes:

> *He is despised and rejected of men; a man of sorrows,*
> *and acquainted with grief: and we hid as it were our*
> *faces from him; he was despised, and we esteemed*
> *him not. Surely, he hath borne our griefs, and carried*
> *our sorrows: yet we did esteem him stricken, smitten*
> *of God, and afflicted.*[76]

Maybe you missed it, but the passage reads that He was *"acquainted with grief"*, and *"he hath borne our griefs."* That tells me that when Jesus was on earth, He too entered into the human experience of enduring losses in a sin ravaged world. He gave himself time to grieve over those losses. Moreover, He came for the express purpose of *"carrying our griefs."* The cross that Jesus carried up Golgotha is a concrete symbol of all the sin losses of this world—*"Surely he has borne our griefs."* He carried the weight of it all on His shoulder, by choice.

The Personal Element of Loss

Each day that we live, we are confronted with losses in this world. It is not the way God intended; it is the result of sin. None of us gets to be a judge of what should be considered a loss for someone else. Each of us experiences loss at a deeply personal level.

Often when an older person dies, there is the expectation that one should perhaps grieve less. After all, they had "a good life." These words often greet mourners over the loss of an elderly parent or grandparent. However, when a child dies, then there is the understanding that the loss is more severe.

I do not agree with this rationale. There is no getting comfortable with death. Loss was never a part of God's plan for us, and it is almost impossible to quantify. When we experience loss, death or otherwise, we must give ourselves permission to grieve the loss.

The loss of the job offer to be a senior administrator was heavy for me. Given my background and upbringing, I never expected that I would be able to pursue higher education, or even aspire to a senior administrative role in a prestigious higher education institution. But God had shown me that vision for my life, and He had walked me through door after door to see that *it was* possible. And so, the loss was hurtful. It made me question my own achievements and self-worth. It made me question people and the entire job search process. I lost some of my naiveté that the most qualified person should be the one who gets the job. It was a loss for the work I knew I was capable of doing in that position and the impact I could have made. It was an attack at my hope for future aspirations. I had serious questions for God about what had happened and what were the lessons He wanted me to learn from this experience. I was angry and confused, so I chose to grieve. Choosing to acknowledge our losses and the emotions that accompany them, is the first step in getting through our brook experience.

Grief is personal and it is up to the individual who has experienced the loss to define and shape the contours of that loss and the grieving experience. Whether it seems to you or me that it is an insignificant thing to grieve over is beside the point. That is not for us to decide.

When you arrive at your brook experience, the first thing that needs to happen during the waiting period is that you need to acknowledge that loss. Name it if you will. What losses are you experiencing as a result of this waiting period? How do those losses make you feel? Journal about it. Take some time out and process what this loss means to you personally. Cry if you must. It might be helpful to talk to a mentor, a friend, or a spiritual advisor about it. However, in some cases, you might also need professional help through the service of grief counseling. There is nothing wrong with doing all that is needed to process the mental and emotional havoc of trauma on our lives. In fact, there is everything right about it. God does not expect us to white knuckle it through the pain. There are no extra brownie points for toughing it out.

We need to get the help we need to process the losses that scar us in this broken world. We need to give ourselves permission to grieve over our losses, and take the time we need to process and to begin to heal.

∞∞∞

Loss was never a part of God's plan for us, and it is almost impossible to quantify. When we experience loss, death or otherwise, we must give ourselves permission to grieve the loss.

Chapter 7. Step 2: Wrestle with God

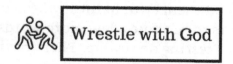
Wrestle with God

The Flight Home

In October 2004, I sat on an American Airlines flight headed to Trinidad from JFK, New York. This should have been a happy trip, but it was not. I was traveling home to bury my father. As I sat there, I kept replaying in my mind the devastating news I had received a few days earlier. On my way back from an academic conference in Harrisburg, Pennsylvania, I made a quick stop at the office to get some books and papers that I needed to take home that weekend. The message light on my office phone was blinking; my sister in Trinidad had left me a message to call her back. Absentmindedly, I reached for the phone with one hand while trying to find a book that I had come to retrieve with my other hand.

When my sister did pick up, I started babbling. I told her about my trip and that I had stopped at the office briefly on my way home. It took me a minute or so to notice the awkward silence at the end of the line. When I finally stopped chattering long enough to ask what was wrong—the silence lengthened. Then, she sighed heavily, and in a tone that was more of an anguish than spoken words she said: "I don't even know how to tell you this . . . sigh . . . Daddy, died last night." There was a long pause as the meaning of those four words sank in. Then across the lines our hearts united in an extended and agonizing sob.

The words, "Daddy died last night," kept playing over and over in my head as I looked out the window through eyes brimmed with tears. I had requested my usual window seat, and I sat huddled against the window pane trying valiantly to write down my recollections about Dad between bouts of crying. Every now and then, I would lift my head off the pane and resume my efforts to scribble a few more words on the yellow notepad that was resting on my lap. Then inevitably the tears would start to fall again, and I would return my head to its leaning spot against the window. I was looking out at clouds but not even able to see them through the thickness of my grief.

Dad was diagnosed with prostate cancer in 2000, and later with Parkinson's disease. After that, his health continued to fail. Since migrating to the United States in 2000 to complete doctoral studies, I was not able to visit him as much as I liked though we did talk often on the phone.

I completed my dissertation in late June of 2004, too late to walk for the May graduation, but I was scheduled to do so the following year. The months prior to my dissertation defense and shortly thereafter were a blur of activities—many late nights trying to get every "i" dotted on my dissertation, then job applications and interviews, and processing the paperwork necessary for approval to complete the one-year optional training offered to immigrant students. I was successful in securing a tenure track job offer at a small liberal arts university with a mid-August start date. The hoped-for trip to Trinidad to celebrate with my dad would have to wait until December, or so I thought.

The loss of my dad at this time in my life was almost unbearable. It saddens me that he died before we could celebrate in our characteristic way. Perhaps both of us sitting in the gallery of the house where I had grown up. I pictured him sitting on his makeshift stool, and I on the banister. We would be looking out at the road and cars going by, and intermittently calling out greetings to neighbors as they passed by on the street. Then he would ask me questions about my professors, and courses and what it was like to live abroad. And I would paint pictures for him about American life and foods, and smog and snow and places he had never been. Ah, to think of it now, still makes my eyes water. He would have loved it.

After the funeral services were completed and I had sorted through what needed to be done with my father's meagre possessions, I made my way back to the US. It was then that a deep and abiding grief enveloped me for the next several months. Many days I could not drag myself out of bed; I had difficulty sleeping, and I ached all over. Eventually, I ended up at the doctor's office where I was diagnosed with fibromyalgia—a condition that causes pain, sleep problems, and fatigue, often brought on by stressful or traumatic events. I was processing through my grief. I was missing my dad. But just below the layer of pain the questions began to surface: God, how can you leave me motherless and fatherless too? Why now? Why would you allow this to happen to me, just so close to sharing this important life milestone with my dad?

Arriving at Questions

Death of a loved one can represent one of the most difficult brook experiences to navigate. No one needs to tell us to give in to grief because the loss can be so overwhelming. A vibrant living presence in our life is now reduced to memories. In some cases, as with "Mom," the brook experience began for us in that month-long agonizing hospital vigil as we prayed for a healthy recovery for her. That waiting continued after she passed, as we tried to process and make sense of this hole in our lives that had been left void. How would it ever be filled again? Could it be filled again? How would we rearrange the threads of our lives around the fabric of holiday meals, baby showers, and birthday parties that she had so masterfully designed? How would we manage to remain connected to each other without her stabilizing presence? More than this, however, we waited for an answer from God that would provide clarity about His will and purpose in all of this.

Loss of any kind, whether through death or some other personal loss, touches the Christian believer in a different way than most. Ultimately, however we choose to get through it, we end up at the place where the loss puts our relationship with God to the test. We begin to wonder, and even question: If God is so good and so kind, if he is leading us through life, if he indeed wants the best for us, how can he allow us to suffer this —loss of hope, crushed expectations, death, struggle to find a mate, struggle to conceive, struggle to get that job offer, lack of financial security, diagnosis of a terminal illness, life-threatening surgery, difficult relationship; abandonment by our parents, rape and/or sexual abuse, divorce....and on and on? And though we know that the world is broken and sin has corrupted His perfect plan for us, these crises provoke questions that impact our continuing trust in Him. The underlying question becomes, "Can we trust God?"

In the months that followed my return from Trinidad, after burying my dad, questions circled in my mind as I waited on God. As I look back on it now, I cannot credit myself with the insight that I now have about what needed to happen for me to get past grief to the other side. I was moving on emotions and instinct, but I do believe that a loving and gracious God was leading me through the process that would allow me to enter into this next act of waiting.

Questioning Our Way Through

Can you doubt your way into faith? When I was in graduate school at a small Christian University in Michigan, I remember taking the course, Philosophy of Christian Education, and the professor posed this question to the class. My response then, and one which I still hold to now is that the question needs to be rephrased. The question is not if we can doubt our way into faith, but "Can we question our way into faith?" The Bible shows us that: "Yes, we can! However, too often we equate questioning with doubting. Or we see doubting as the antithesis of faith. The example of the blind man before Jesus wanting to believe but recognizing his own inability to come to the thing he most wants, is an encouragement to us all —we can question God, we can even come to him with a shaky, kind of faith that is mingled with seeds of doubt and cry out like the blind man as recorded in Mark 9:24: "I do believe, but help me overcome my unbelief!"

As we make our way through our grief and the losses that have brought us to our brook experience, we find ourselves with questions for God that seem improper to ask. The reason they may seem improper to ask is because that is not how most of us have been socialized to prayer. I certainly was not. In fact, if we listen to the prayers that are prayed from most pulpits at church, we might come to think of those prayers as representing the standard template of prayer; we might come to view any deviation from this template as sacrosanct.

However, when we approach God in prayer, we have been given the privilege to talk to Him as we would to a "Daddy" who is eager to converse with His children. We do not approach our earthly fathers with one kind of conversation template, do we? No, we don't. We have several. For example, our conversations with them can center around making requests, expressing thankfulness, seeking clarity about something that is happening to us or in the world around us, and sometimes even lodging a complaint to them. In the same way, we can come to our Heavenly Father with different types of prayers based on differing needs.

Here are just a few examples of prayers that step unapologetically outside expected liturgical boundaries. When Abraham learns that God is going to destroy Sodom and Gomorrah as recorded in Genesis 18:23: (NLT), he enters into a negotiation with God to save the city if a few righteous are found there, and God agrees to the conditions requested by Abraham. "*Abraham approached him and said, "Will you sweep away both the righteous and the wicked? "*

In many of the psalms, like Psalm 13:1-3 (NIV), we see the psalmist earnestly questioning God: *"How long, O LORD? Will you forget me forever? How long will you hide your face from me? How long must I wrestle with my thoughts and every day have sorrow in my heart? "* Then again in Psalm 42: 9-10: *"I say to God my Rock,"Why have you forgotten me? Why must I go about mourning, oppressed by the enemy?" My bones suffer mortal agony as my foes taunt me, saying to me all day long, "Where is your God?"*

Job also questions God in his suffering in Job 7: 20-21, (NIV):

> *If I have sinned, what have I done to you,*
> *you who see everything we do?*
> *Why have you made me your target?*
> *Have I become a burden to you?*
> *Why do you not pardon my offenses*
> *and forgive my sins?*

What these prayers illustrate is that God is not offended by the questionings of His children. Rather, I suggest that He delights in this kind of relational exchange with us because it is the path to deeper intimacy within the relationship.

It is in times of great distress, fear, loss, and anger that we are most in a place to talk with God from a heart stripped free of much of the pretense and liturgical flourish that accompany communication with Him in seasons of plenty. It is in this period of waiting that we must bring those questions to God. We can remind Him of His promises to us, and question Him about how much longer we need to wait. It is here we can express our disappointment, pain and grief to a father who cares for us. Here we can ask Him earnestly for the answers that we seek.

Jacob Questions God

Jacob finds himself in this place of questioning God one night. He is desperate for answers. God had told Jacob to return to his father's house, yet on the way there, he receives news from his messengers that his brother Esau is on his way to meet him with a militia of 400 men. Jacob had left his home many years prior because of his own deception. He had tricked his father into blessing him rather than the rightful first born, his brother, Esau. Now about twenty years later he is returning in obedience to God. But he is afraid. He is unsure about how his brother will receive him. The news that Esau is headed in his direction with a small army of men fills him with dread. Maybe Jacob wonders, "Why would God allow me to return home and have Esau attack me?" Jacob is perplexed about the workings of God. And so, he prays to God: *"Then Jacob prayed, "O God of my grandfather Abraham, and God of my father, Isaac O Lord, you told me, 'Return to your own land and to your relatives.' And you promised me, 'I will treat you kindly.'"*[77] Jacob reminds God of what He promised. Did you get that? Jacob is saying to God, "You promised me... You are the one who told me to return, God? So, what's up, God? My brother is coming to kill me? But you promised!"

I imagine Jacob's voice has the tone of one of my daughter's reminding me about something that I promised to do, which I have long since forgotten, and I have not done. Being forgetful of what one has promised is evidence of human frailty. But does the all-powerful God need reminding? Isn't it rude of Jacob to presume to remind God about His promises? Apparently, not! God does not seem to think so, because He is listening. So, Jacob continues to persist in prayer. He sends his messengers with gifts for Esau, then he sends his wives and his children and his possessions over to the other side of the Jabbok River, and he remains behind alone because he has business to do with God.

It is around midnight. I imagine Jacob is kneeling in prayer. He continues to remind God of what He promised, and he pleads with Him to change Esau's intention towards him. Suddenly, he feels the grip of an unfamiliar arm on his shoulder. In the darkness, he cannot tell who it is. Perhaps, he thinks, "It is Esau coming to attack me by surprise!" Instinctively, he puts up the fight of his life. Jacob "wrestled with an Angel."[78]

Who was this person? Various interpretations have been offered about the identity of this midnight visitor. Some say that he was the "Angel of the Covenant,"[79] Christ himself. Others suggest that he was an angel messenger from God.[80] Jacob tries in vain to inquire about the identity of his assailant without success. What is clear is that Jacob is having an encounter with divinity—for the angel touched Jacob's hip and it is dislocated.

Wrestling with God

This image of Jacob wrestling through the night with God's messenger is iconic. It illustrates beautifully how each of us must wrestle with God as we wait by our brook. Jacob wrestles with God on the other side of the Jabbok river. He wrestles with God, alone. He wrestles with God until dawn. He wrestles with God until he gets the answer to his request. There is so much that happens in this midnight to morning encounter that is instructive about how we can process through our grief to get to the other side of the brook.

On a very human level, we need to address the emotional and psychological residuals that accompany our loss. As discussed in the previous chapter, Step 1 is to acknowledge the loss and deal with the emotions that accompany that loss. However, getting over the trauma of loss at the psychological level is only the first stage of the journey. We must also address the trauma that this loss inflicts on our connection to God.

Here at the Jabbok river, Jacob is making his way through that important spiritual trauma as he "wrestles" it out with God. As deep as the implications of this aspect of the encounter is, there is a clear reality that is just as important. This is an intimate and physical confrontation. Two beings grapple with each other through the night. Can you see them struggling, twisting and turning every which way trying to pin each other down to the ground? The imagery is gripping. This is an intense struggle; it is also a persistent encounter. Jacob is not willing to give up. His mission with God has been interrupted, but not terminated. When he finds out to his amazement that the one with whom he is wrestling has the capacity to grant the very petitions for which he has been praying, he makes his request directly: "*I will not let You go unless You bless me.*"[81]

Jacob's wrestling with God at Jabbok is a fitting metaphor for the encounter with God to which we must all aspire to get through our brook experience. It is an encounter in which we come to God alone in prayer and anguish, often in the darkness of night, and we talk to Him with the full potency of the emotions that accompany our loss—pain, frustration, hurt, anger, lingering questions. Don't worry. God can take it. He delights in this kind of one-on-one exchange. He wants us to come to Him earnestly seeking answers about the challenges we have experienced in our lives. The beauty of these meetings is that they are personal—they are between you and God. What happens with you and God by the brook, stays by the brook.

You may be wondering: "How long should I stay by the brook wrestling with God?" The answer is: "As long as it takes for your humanity to have an intimate encounter with divinity!" But make no mistake, this kind of relationship building with God is not for the faint of heart. This is not the kind of knee sweeping prayer that gets you through the minor hurdles of life. This is the kind of spiritual experience that has left me in tears. This is a kind of "snot running down my nose, crying out in anguish, mumbling words over and over again in incoherent speech, don't-even-know-how-long-I-have-been -praying" kind of prayer. This is crazy prayer. It is the kind of praying that I believe Hannah was doing in the temple when Eli thought she was drunk. And yet, I have come to realize that this is the kind of prayer that moves the heart of God. The Spirit takes our groanings and the imperfect utterings from a broken heart[82] and presents them to the Father, and they are like a sweet fragrance in His presence.

As surely as Jacob leaves that encounter with a physical reminder of that night—the messenger touches Jacob's hip and wrenches it out of its socket—we do not leave that encounter the same. When we wrestle through this experience, we will receive a blessing from our time here. However, like Jacob, to get there, we must experience a new depth of brokenness and surrender.

∞∞∞

This is the kind of prayer that moves the heart of God. The Spirit takes our groanings and the imperfect utterings from a broken heart and presents them to the Father, and they are like a sweet fragrance in His presence.

Chapter 8. Step 3: Pivot to Praise

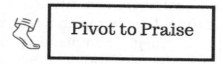

Hannah's Dilemma

On this day that Hannah slips away from her family to go into the temple, she is desperate. Today, she is determined. Like Jacob at Jabbok, she is not going to let go until God blesses her with the son for whom she has been praying. Can you see her making her way inside? She is a bit weary but still determined. When she gets there, she enters into a heartfelt conversation with God. I see this woman of faith so engrossed in communion with her God that she is oblivious to all else around her.

Hannah had experienced loss and grief for many years. I can identify with her. I remember my own experience hoping for our first child. Mark and I married late in life, so in the first year of marriage I can still recall the deep longing for that first sign that the miracle of conception had happened. But month after month that joyful hope would end in disappointment— the pregnancy strip would not show the hoped-for plus sign. I grieved the loss of what could have been—the start of a new life. I grieved the loss of yet another month in the journey to motherhood with time running out for us and the possibility of having children of our own. How many months had Hannah been through that experience? Had she also experienced miscarriages? How many months, even years had she endured the accompanying taunts of an unkind sister wife who went to great pains to make her life miserable.

When the story of her plight opens up in 1 Samuel 1, Hannah is in the midst of distress over her infertility. She has lost her appetite and weeps constantly. It is during this time that she chooses to slip away and have another one-on-one meeting with God. She has been positioned beside her brook for a long time, but I imagine that there is a different level of urgency in her prayers this time. I see her with a tear-stained face expressing her pain and struggle, complaining to God, and even bargaining with Him. She is so intent in her petitioning that she fails to realize that she is not alone. The high priest Eli enters, sees her antics, and assumes that she is drunk. It might be that Hannah's lips are moving, but no sounds are coming out.[83] Maybe she is wandering around on wobbly feet on the verge of falling down, or she is making wild arm and hand gestures as she converses with an invisible presence. Whether her movements are some or all of the above, this is not a woman who is drunk. This is a woman who is wrestling it out with God in prayer. Hannah convinces Eli that she is not drunk. She shares her prayer request with him, and he promises to also pray for her.

Here in the temple, she is about to experience a change in her mindset; it is here that she makes a dramatic turn. She begins her pivot from lament into praise. She leaves the temple comforted and filled with hope: "*Then she went back and began to eat again, and she was no longer sad.*"[84] Through her petition and the assurance of the high priest Eli, she accepts by faith that her prayer has been answered affirmatively—God will grant her a child.

The Pivot

If you have ever played basketball or you are a fan, you will be familiar with the word "pivot." In the field of sports where the term originated, the pivot is a masterful move that allows a player to rotate or move around with one foot while using the other foot to stay steady. The pivot is defined as the act of keeping one foot in place "the pivot foot" while moving the other to allow one to reposition oneself legally in a game.

The phrase has increased in common usage even outside sports. Content creators and marketing experts use the word "pivot" to describe the moves that startups often make to remain agile and competitive in the marketplace. If one strategy does not work, the company pivots or moves to another strategy. What is interesting about the pivot is that it is not an "all or nothing" move. To make the move, it is not necessary to move both feet at the same time. The pivot foot remains stationary, while the player or company is able to make a repositioning move that is necessary for advancement.

The expression "pivoting into praise" captures well the move we must make during and after we have wrestled with God for the answers we seek. In every instance in which I have wrestled with God to seek answers for some of the losses or delays in my life, I have found myself often straddling the line between questioning and even complaining to God one minute (the pivot foot), even as I have tried to reposition myself into praise and trust.

Scripture also shows us many occasions when those who walked closely with God found themselves in positions of grief and complaint even as they attempted to follow God. The entire book of Lamentations is an example of one long lament. The prophet Habakkuk also expressed his pain and grief over the judgment that was about to come upon Israel. Even Jesus pleaded to His father in the Garden of Gethsemane to spare Him the suffering that He was about to endure while simultaneously expressing His trust in the Father's will.[85]

In addition, the book of Psalms offers some of the most moving sacred verses or hymns that express deep sorrow, grief and sometimes regret. Altogether, these kinds of psalms, called lament psalms, make up the largest category in the book, accounting for about one-third of the psalms. In this type of verse, we see expressions of human struggle presented to God with a plea for help in community[86] or individually.[87] Each of these lament psalms is a study in how we can move from complaining/questioning to pivoting into praise.

Lament psalms share the following common characteristics:[88]

Crying Out to God. The psalmist cries out to God expressing the depths of their pain. These prayers are void of pretense. A lament psalm is the earnest and honest cry of the soul sometimes questioning, complaining and in deep despair: *"I am weary with my moaning; every night I flood my bed with tears; I drench my couch with my weeping."*[89]

Asking for Help. The psalmist turns to God and asks for help to overcome the pain and/or that God will respond to and meet their needs, *"O God, be not far from me; O my God, make haste to help me!"*[90]

Pivoting to Praise. Through the process of the lament: first, crying out to God and expressing their emotions around grief and loss, then asking God for help, the psalmist eventually surrenders to God and arrives at a place of praise and trust. The path to getting there involves reflecting on the ways in which God has blessed them in the past and expressing gratitude for past blessings in the midst of brokenness: *"I give thanks to you, O Lord my God, with my whole heart, and I will glorify your name forever."*[91]

However, the process of getting to surrender is a gradual one. Though it might seem that the psalmist arrived at praise quickly through a number of verses, it is most likely that these psalms reflect an extended chronology of time expressed in poetic form.

The path to surrender took Jacob into the wee hours of the morning, while it took Hannah perhaps a few hours in the temple. There is no standard time frame for surrender. You do it for as long as it takes, no one should force you based on their timetable. Ignore the well-wishers who try to get you there before you are ready. Rushing to get there is a mistake. At the same time, it is while we continue to wrestle with God that we must prepare ourselves to use this positioning as our base from which we can rotate into a position of praise.

Moving to Surrender

As we wrestle with God, each of us will come to a point of surrender. Do we surrender to God our Maker or do we surrender to the inclinations of our own hearts? That is really what the struggle is about. As God reveals His will and purpose in our brook experience, we are faced with a choice to arrive at the place of surrender and complete brokenness before Him or to decide to do things our way. For Paul, this moment of surrender was wrapped up in his acceptance that the *"thorn in his flesh,"* whatever it was, would be a lifelong battle—it was not going away.[92] For David, it was the death of his first son after he had asked God to spare the child's life.[93] For Jacob, it was the calm assurance that God would take care of him as He had promised.[94] This is the place where we can come to acknowledge and accept like Job that He is God, and He is in control.

However, if we choose to surrender to God, it will require a masterful move—the pivot. For often as we strive to come to an acceptance of God's sovereignty in our affairs, we may still feel hurt that what God has allowed us to go through has come at too great a cost—it appears to be a Pyrrhic[95] victory. We exist in a space of tension between struggle and surrender. This is the place that the pivoting metaphor is most appropriate. In spite of the losses which may remain present with us for a long time (that steady foot), we begin to reposition ourselves (the other foot) so that we can continue to advance in the direction of God's leading in our lives. The key to making this move is to reflect on and rely on what we know about God and past victories.

We know that God is good! We can arrive at the place of surrender because of this calm assurance. We can trust God! The evidence is all around us! We have seen evidence of His goodness in this created world which He has given us to enjoy. We see evidence of His provisions in our life every time we breathe in and out, every time light enters our eyes and we are able to behold the beauty of color, and the beauty of the world. Every time we look into the eyes of children and marvel at the miracle of new life in them, we see evidence of God's goodness.

His track record of taking care of us is solid! And though we may not ever be able to see His divine workings behind this painful chapter in our life this side of the journey, we can be confident that "*God causes everything to work together for the good of those who love God and are called according to his purpose for them.*"[96] For example, I know that God's perfect plan for my life did not involve hurt and death and pain, but in this sin infected world, loss happens to us all. But a good and loving God weaves the dark threads of loss into the golden tapestry design He has for my life to create a masterpiece. It is with this understanding that we can move to surrender in the midst of lament and then on to praise.

Moving from Surrender to Praise

In the field of positive psychology, researchers spend much time studying the science behind happiness. Are there strategies we can adopt that will enable us to live happy lives? In the book, *The How of Happiness*, professor of psychology Sonja Lyubomirsky[97] presents an interesting finding about the path to cultivating happiness. While it is commonly believed that our circumstances play a significant role in our overall happiness, a strong body of research on happiness[98] suggests otherwise. Interestingly, the breakdown of factors that contribute to our overall happiness is as follows: circumstances contribute 10%; set point genetics contribute 50%; and intentional activity contributes 40%. What these data show is that our ability to be happy is largely a function of intentional action that we take. Chief among those factors is adopting a spirit of gratitude.[99]

John Milton put it this way: "The mind is its own place, and in itself/Can make a Heaven of Hell, a Hell of Heaven."[100]

But we do not need scientists or poets to tell us this. The Bible has many passages that remind us of the power of positive thinking and choosing to rejoice in spite of our circumstances. However, if you are anything like me, you might have muttered under your breath as you read scriptural passages that tell us to "Rejoice at all times!"—"Sure that's easy for you to say!"

I will just admit that in some of my darker moments, when I could not shake the mindset that a particular life challenge was not preparation but punishment, I have wondered whether such advice is a way to placate us so that we will not think of God as unfair or unjust. Yes, I have. But what I have come to realize as I have lived through the pain of delay or loss while trying to reconcile my questionings about why a good God would allow me to suffer so, is that choosing gratitude in the face of life challenges is not a mantra for working ourselves into delusion about our current state of affairs. Rather, it is the prescription for the cure.

A few years ago, I listened to renowned minister Rick Warren and his wife Kay recount the experience of losing their son. They told the story of a young man tormented by mental illness. In spite of their prayers and the many steps they took to get him the help he needed, he eventually succumbed to his illness and took his life one fateful day. And yes, Rick and his wife struggled through this brook experience that spanned the lifetime of their son—and then his death, but they chose to praise God through the circumstances.

Anyone who has experienced this kind of loss would know that the grief is not a "one and done deal." Instead, it is a daily commitment and intentional choice to live in the space of gratitude while we wait. Notice, I said it is a choice. We may not feel like it, but we do it anyhow. Yes! One of the biggest mistakes we can make at this phase of our brook experience is to wait until our praise is perfected to offer it up. This is like waiting until you feel better to take the medication.

There are other misconceptions about the purpose of praise in our relationship with God. If we view God as a monarch who demands that His subjects praise and remind Him of His goodness over and over again so that He can bless them, we have a wrong understanding of the purpose of praise in the Christian experience. Listen, God does not require our praise to bless us. The Bible tells us that *"He gives His sunlight to both the evil and the good, and he sends rain on the just and the unjust alike."*[101] Praising God is not about finding the right word or phrase which will magically unlock the blessings He has for us. In fact, even the very best praise we can offer God is imperfect because we are sinful. Heavenly angels who have never sinned bow down day and night before God giving Him perfect praise: *"Day and night they never stop saying: '"Holy, holy, holy is the Lord God Almighty."*[102]

So why are we expected to *"Bless the Lord at all times"*, and to let *"His praise continually be in our mouths?"*[103] Why are we told: *"when troubles of any kind come your way, consider it an opportunity for great joy."*[104]? Here's one reason why—praise benefits us! In the midst of our lament and our pain, even as we continue to wrestle with God, we can offer up imperfect praise—it is the bridge that will get us to the other side. If we are waiting —too afraid to offer up our "watery" praise, we will not get to the other side of the brook experience. Praise is the pathway to healing; it is the vehicle that can transport us out of suffering and into joy.

Notice I said joy and not happiness. Joy is a very different thing from happiness. Yet if you browse through any book of positive psychology you will often see the words "joy" and "happiness" used interchangeably. However, whereas happiness is connected to things and circumstances "joy" is experienced in relation to a being—God.[105] Joy is an elevated way of being in the world that is in sync with living a life that connects us to the Divine. Unlike happiness, joy is a way of interacting with difficult circumstances in our life that seems counterintuitive to the prescriptions for happiness. Joy allows us to think of the misfortune—our lost job, or lost house, diagnosis of a terminal illness, or a broken relationship as "good." Sounds crazy, right? But according to Miroslav Volf, Founder and Executive Director of the Yale Center for Faith and Culture, "joy is tied to how I perceive things rather than to what things are in themselves."[106] Hence, we develop the ability to praise God in the midst of pain and suffering and experience joy. The only way we are able to achieve and live in this elevated state of being in the world is as we deepen our connection to God.

Praise Him for the Brook

God invites us to cultivate a spirit of gratitude while we wait. However, it is important that we navigate Steps 1 and 2 to position ourselves here where we can pivot into praise. Even while we are still struggling to make sense of all that has happened, we begin to turn in the direction of gratitude and praise. Most likely we are not going to be fully positioned to rejoice in our circumstances the first time. That pivot foot may remain grounded in questioning and lament for quite some time. But we know the direction in which we need to go, so we begin to rotate out of complaint into full surrender and praise.

Here is the thing about expressing gratitude—it is one of those superpower activities that transforms our perspective as we practice it. If you decide in this moment to think about all the things for which you are grateful, it is as though you begin to peel back the dark cloud on an overcast sky and before you know it the sun is shining through.

I know of what I speak because even at the time of writing this, I still wonder and question God about the purpose of the many losses and delays I have experienced over the last several years. I still lack complete clarity about His will and purpose in these experiences, but whenever I find myself going down that old rabbit hole, I make a conscious choice to pivot into praise even if all I can give Him is a "Broken Hallelujah."[107]

The most challenging and important praise that we can

bring to our waiting season is to praise Him in the midst of the wait! Express gratitude to God for even your brook experience! When we are in the place where we can do this, we are positioned to benefit from even this season of our life. We are ready to focus on the lessons that this particular experience has to teach us. We can begin to appreciate that time spent beside the brook is not punishment but preparation for what lies ahead.

∞∞∞

Praise is the pathway to healing; it is the vehicle that can transport us out of suffering and into joy.

Chapter 9. Step 4: Develop in Darkness

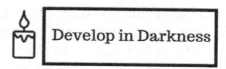

Develop in Darkness

Hidden in Prison

For years, Rachel, like Hannah, has suffered through the agony of barrenness. While her prayers to God for a son go unanswered, her sister Leah it seems gives birth to another son every Monday morning. Finally, *"God remembered Rachel's plight and answered her prayers by enabling her to have children."*[108] She bears a son and calls him Joseph. Her joy can almost not be contained, and it pours itself out in indulgence for her miracle child. Joseph is doted on by his mother and loved by his father Jacob as the first son born to the wife he loves most.

However, Joseph's idyllic childhood is about to come to an abrupt end. Rachel dies giving birth to his brother Benjamin when Joseph is just about seven years old. His father, Jacob, unwisely favors Joseph, above his other children with catastrophic results. We are told that *"Jacob loved Joseph more than any of his other children because Joseph had been born to him in his old age."*[109]

I imagine that long before Joseph's brothers devise the wicked plan to get rid of him, their resentment has been brewing. It is clear to them from the day Joseph is born, that he will occupy a favored spot in their father's heart. As if that is not enough, Joseph has two dreams which suggest that one day he will rule over them all. What? Joseph is not the eldest! In Jewish culture, that position rightly belongs to the eldest, Reuben, the son of Leah. Their resentment grows: *"But his brothers hated Joseph because their father loved him more than the rest of them. They couldn't say a kind word to him."*[110]

Maybe in spite of all of this, they try their best to ignore it or to live with the understanding that they will not occupy that coveted position of affection in their father's eyes. But when Jacob presents young Joseph with a fancy coat which none of them have been given, it is more than they can bear. And so, one day their bitterness towards Joseph turns into action. They throw Joseph into a pit, and then sell him to Ishmaelite slave traders. This singular action sets in motion an extended series of trying brook experiences for young Joseph.

The slave traders take Joseph to Egypt, where he is bought to serve in the house of one of the most important men in Egypt—Potiphar. Joseph, the favorite and over-indulged son, becomes Joseph the slave. Joseph now occupies the lowest of statuses in this household. But even here, *"the Lord was with Joseph, so he succeeded in everything he did as he served in the home of his Egyptian master."*[111] Joseph works diligently, and his hard work and commitment are noted by Potiphar. It is not long before he is recognized as a most valued slave and becomes Potiphar's personal attendant. In spite of this apparent rise in status, Joseph is still a slave. He is still miles away from his family. He still misses his mother and father, and he is still perhaps confused about why God is allowing him to be in the predicament in which he finds himself in Egypt. However, Joseph's brook experience is just beginning.

In addition to all Joseph has going for him, he is a handsome young man. His good looks soon catch the eyes of Potiphar's wife. However, her plans to seduce him fail miserably, and her deceptive accusations that it was Joseph who attempted to abuse her, lands Joseph in prison for a crime he did not commit. But again, even here, *"the Lord was with Joseph in the prison and showed him His faithful love. And the Lord made Joseph a favorite with the prison warden."*[112] Joseph's diligent work once again allows him to rise in the ranks until he is appointed as the chief prison warden.

And so, Joseph waits in prison. However, even while he waits for the fulfillment of God's promise in his life, he does the work before him, and he does it well. He lives the admonition: *"Do you see any truly competent workers? They will serve kings rather than working for ordinary people."*[113]

While he is in prison, he helps two prisoners interpret troubling dreams.[114] These inmates are not common men. They serve in Pharaoh's court. One is the chief baker and the other is the cupbearer for Pharaoh. Joseph correctly interprets their dreams which tell of coming events—and it happens just as he said. The baker dies, but the cupbearer—the one who serves Pharaoh directly—returns to serve Pharaoh once again. However, before the cupbearer leaves prison, Joseph sees an opportunity for his release through this connection he has made to Pharaoh's ear; he asks the cupbearer to plead with Pharaoh for his release from prison. But once the cupbearer is out of prison he *"forgot all about Joseph, never giving it another thought."*[115] Joseph would have to wait two more years until the cupbearer remembered the name Joseph and his ability to interpret dreams.

Preparation Time

In reading the story of Joseph hidden away in prison, we may miss the full extent of the emotional and mental cost to him during that time. What must it have been like for Joseph to have the gift of leadership bound up within him, only to be hidden away for so many years? What must it have been like for him to have a vision for an elevated status and be demoted to the positions of slave and prisoner? While he was still a boy in his father's camp, God had shown him a vision for his life. One day his entire family would bow down before him. He would rule over them. It was a position of leadership and of rulership. But when would that day come? The path to that day was full of injustice against him and long periods of waiting unsure of when his arduous journey would end. The path to that day would see him thrown into a pit by his own brothers. The path to that day would land him as a slave in an Egyptian household. The path to that day would take him into the recesses of a dark and putrid prison dungeon. What Joseph did not know was that the path to the fulfillment of his dream went straight through his prison cell.

Joseph faced brook experience after brook experience. I cannot even begin to put myself in his position. Did he doubt God and the calling on his life during this time? Did he question when God was going to fulfill the dream that He had shown him as a boy? Did Joseph reach a point of frustration and did he cry out and wrestle with God? I cannot help but think that during those many years, Joseph processed through the many emotional stages of grief just as we do, and he too wrestled with God, until he landed in the place of surrender.

I imagine that he wrestled with God to understand the injustice of this situation. I imagine him finally surrendering to God and trusting Him for the journey. In one of my favorite animated interpretations of this story of Joseph, the lyricist interprets Joseph's surrender with the words of this very fitting song titled, "You Know Better Than I."[116] Joseph surrenders to God's sovereign will and in obscurity, he continues to develop the gifts God has placed in him still waiting on God's perfect timing.

Our brooks are not places of resignation; they are places of transition.

Do Not Despise the Small Tasks

When I moved to the United States from the British Virgin Islands to pursue doctoral studies at Temple University, I had to accept a fall in social status. As a student, I could not afford to own a car on a large urban campus. There would be the cost of the car, then the steep cost of car insurance in the city of Philadelphia, then the cost of on campus parking, and on and on —I was barely earning enough money to cover my tuition and living expenses. In the BVI, I was in the position of authority in a classroom as an instructor. In the Office of the Dean in the College of Education at Temple University, I was a graduate assistant—a fancy term for a "go-fer". Many times, I felt discouraged about my new status in life and what came with it.

I distinctly remember one night when I was waiting for the bus, and it was snowing a dribbling kind of snow; the snow turned into water as it fell and the coldness of it seemed to penetrate my coat and suck out the last bit of Caribbean sunshine I had left in me. I was wet and cold. But more than feeling cold, I was miserable. As I stood there waiting on the bus that seemed like it would never come, I could see people driving by in their cars sipping what I assumed was hot chocolate and chatting and laughing with one another, and I felt absolutely sorry for myself. It was the end of one of the evenings where I had to complete a task in my role as a graduate assistant. This task required me a couple of evenings a week to take the subway up Broad Street, then transfer to a bus at Olney station in Philadelphia, and then walk a couple of blocks to and from an after-school program as the program coordinator and eyes and ears of my supervisor. I did this whether it was raining or snowing. It was tedious work, and I could have skipped it or called in sick. But even in that miserable weather and even when I felt tired, I did it.

What I did not even realize at the time was that the skills I was getting there were the very skills that I would need to secure my current job. What I also did not realize was that my supervisor, the Dean of the College of Education, saw how hard I was working and he went out of his way to support me, and write glowing recommendations for me for the position I now occupy.

It was Shakespeare who said, "There is a divinity that shapes our ends, rough hew them how we will."[117] Even though we don't understand the path that is laid out before us, we know Someone who does—God! We must come to the place in the uncertainty of our journey where we trust God's wisdom in using the position where He has currently placed us to prepare us for the ministry that He has ahead of us. Now that I am ahead of many of my own brook experiences, I can see how each one was part of God's master plan for my success.

Similarly, before Joseph rose to the ranks of second in command in Egypt, there were lessons he had to master in the curriculum of being a slave. Was it to teach him humility? Was it so that he could understand the way his brothers might have felt when he was treated as superior to them? One of my favorite Christian authors has written this about Joseph's time of waiting:

> He found work to do even in prison. God was preparing him in the school of affliction for greater usefulness, and he did not refuse the needful discipline. In prison, witnessing the results of oppression and tyranny and the effects of crime, he learned lessons of justice, sympathy and mercy that prepared him to exercise power with wisdom and compassion. [118]

Egypt was preparation time for Joseph. Someone has said that "the thing about opportunity is that it often comes disguised as hard work."

Here's the thing. Isn't it interesting that when you think God is putting you through a difficult brook experience, He really is preparing you to walk into what He has called you to do? He is setting you up for success. The problem is that many of us might completely miss it, if we despise the small tasks on the road to greatness. We might miss it, if we wimp out or we do a mediocre job where God has placed us. What we need to do while we wait is to grow in place! What we need to do is to develop in darkness!

Remember Daniel in Babylon. Daniel was taken away as a young man from the comforts of home to a strange land. Yet Daniel did what was necessary for him to grow in place. And *"then this Daniel was preferred above the presidents and princes, because an excellent spirit was in him; and the king thought to set him over the whole realm."*[119] Daniel followed the admonition of the wise man: *"Whatever your hand finds to do, do it with all your might."*[120] This was also the motto of Joseph the slave and prisoner who rose to be king. This was the motto of David, the shepherd boy who became king! On your way to becoming king, before you put on the crown, you are not too big to shovel sheep poop. You are not too important to sweep the floor, clean the bathroom, to do the small tasks in front of you.

Today, I can write the letters Ph.D. after my name, but let me tell you that along the path to getting that degree I learned like the shepherd boy David to be an excellent "sheep poop shoveler". I learned not to despise the small tasks.

Developing in Darkness

One of the most pernicious misconceptions about brook experience is that our job here is to simply wait. If we adopt this mindset, we will abuse this time of waiting by the brook. So how should we wait? The idea of developing in darkness requires us to do several things in preparation for the journey ahead. Waiting by the brook is not a time of dormancy. It is a time of intentional activity!

As you wait in darkness, you are to begin developing the gifts that God has placed within you. After we have grieved our loss, and wrestled with God, we can position ourselves to pivot into praise. It is in this position of gratitude that we can come to accept that even this dark place and time can be useful. God can and will use even this life challenge for His purpose.

I know this from experience. For example, after I did not get the job offer, I spent much time lamenting the loss. I wrestled with God over it. I talked to Mark and other friends who I kept in my circle of trust about it. What happened to me in this space is that I began to think about other possibilities for my life. I came to accept the possibility that maybe my brook experience was not about getting that job at all. What if it was about casting a larger vision for my life than the one I had previously settled for? What if it was an affirmation that God was calling me to a position of greater impact and influence? Suddenly my eyes were opened and I understood what the area of focus was for this juncture in my career path. I also saw with clarity the leadership capabilities within me. It was out of that brook experience that I had my training regimen for what I needed to do while I continued to wait on God.

So, what did I do? I used this time to develop and hone my leadership skills and the gifts God had given me even more by taking on more risks in my personal and professional life. I committed to studying my daughters in depth, and to asking God to reveal their gifts and abilities to me so that I could do everything to nurture them. I wanted them to also be able to dream big, and to trust God for greatness. Why? Because the experience made me realize that I had been thinking too small. I had been limiting myself, when it was clear that I had what it took to make it through the door and into the C-suite.

I also began taking more leadership responsibilities. I applied for leadership positions on boards. I began to focus my research and scholarship efforts more tightly around the topic of women and leadership and diversity and inclusion which I am passionate about.[121] I said "yes" to more opportunities that allowed me to serve on a larger playing field than my institutional base. I accepted a nomination to serve as an elder in my local church. I put in an application to serve on the Mayor's Commission for Faith-based and Interfaith Affairs in the City of Philadelphia. I began working on revamping my blog site and my business teaching people how to navigate life so that they can flourish.[122] And I began writing this book. I took this dark period of ambiguity as the perfect opportunity to develop the gifts within me for the next stop on my journey.

The brook is an excellent preparation ground. In God's preparation plan, a season of obscurity often comes before promotion. Before Joseph could become prime minister, he had to spend time in difficult places away from those he loved learning complete surrender to God. Before Elijah could stand on Mount Carmel, he had to sit by a brook alone with God. He had to spend time with a widow and her son learning about complete dependence on God. There were lessons to be learned during this time that would prepare him for his destiny. Before Moses, could stand before Pharaoh and make the bold proclamation, *"Thus saith the LORD God of the Hebrews, Let my people go, that they may serve me.!,"*[123] he had to learn to corral sheep all alone on the back side of a mountain.[124] Before John the Baptist began his ministry in preparation for Jesus, God was preparing Him in desert places for the gravity and austerity of his life to follow.[125] And before Jesus began His important work that He had come here to do, He spent forty days and nights alone in the desert, fasting and praying.[126] These individuals were being prepared in periods of darkness to develop the gifts inside them for the tasks ahead.

In the same way, your waiting period is preparation time for the next phase of your journey. Don't make the mistake that so many others make of just sitting by idly waiting. God is not your magician in the sky. He has given you gifts and abilities, and a sound mind that is a one of a kind, miraculous, super computer that cannot be duplicated. He expects you to use what He has given you to partner with Him so you can advance towards the great work that He is calling you to do. This is the time to recalibrate, and to refocus. Your stop at the brook is not a vacation. This is not a place of resignation; this is a developing station.

Ask yourself, "What are the lessons that God has for me to learn during this brook experience?" What personal, physical, spiritual, mental, and/or professional skills does he want me to work on developing as I wait?

Then make use of every opportunity to develop those skills that will be needed for the next phase of the journey.

∞∞∞

When you think God is putting you through a difficult brook experience, He really is preparing you to walk into what He has called you to do. He is setting you up for success. The problem is that many of us might completely miss it, if we despise the small tasks on the road to greatness. We might miss it, if we wimp out or we do a mediocre job where God has placed us. What we need to do while we wait—is to grow in place! What we need to do is to develop in darkness!

Chapter 10. Step 5: Encourage Yourself in God

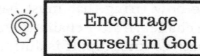

Encourage Yourself in God

A Place Called Ziklag

The story of David's ascension from shepherd boy to King shows well a long progression of challenging brook experiences. You will remember David, the eighth son of Jesse. Bible historians tell us that David was just a boy about fifteen years old when he was anointed to be the next king of Israel by the prophet Samuel. What is admirable about young David is that this anointing towards a great destiny did not seem to affect his willingness to serve with humility. David continued to be the "go-fer" in his family even after God had made the call on his life.

Therefore, it is no surprise that Jesse calls David one day and tells him, *"Here I want you to take some food for your brothers, some roasted grain, and loaves of bread and take some cheeses for the commander of their unit."*[127] In obedience to his father's wishes, David goes to meet his brothers and finds them camped in the Valley of Elah. It is here that he sees God's chosen people —the children of Israel trembling with fear. They are afraid of the Philistines and their champion warrior, a monster of a man called Goliath. David is horrified when he hears Goliath defying the name of God, and he sees that no one else in the Israelite camp will step forward to fight against such blatant disrespect. Well, it is almost more than young David can take, so he says, "*I will fight Goliath!*"[128]

Later, after he has killed Goliath, King Saul becomes jealous of David, and tries on several different occasions to kill him. As a result, David becomes a fugitive and an outlaw. For a period of about eight years, David and Saul are engaged in a battle of wills. Saul is pursuing David to kill him, and David has to keep himself on the move to avoid being killed.

Can you imagine how tiring that must have been? These years are filled with challenge after challenge for David and his men—still on the path to kingship. It is during this time that David faces one of the most difficult points in his journey yet! The account is recorded in 1-Samuel 30:1-6.

Here is the full chronology of events. King Achish of the Philistines has asked David to fight with him against the Israelites. But David does not want to fight against his own people even though King Saul is intent on killing him, and he is able to get out of this duty through his cunning and reliance on God. After these negotiations, David and his men travel back to their camp. It is a journey of about fifty miles and takes them three days. And so, they enter the camp weary from their travels only to find that the unthinkable has happened. David and his men find the camp burned down, the women and children gone, and their supplies stolen.

> *Now when David and his men came to Ziklag on the third day, the Amalekites had made a raid against the Negeb and against Ziklag. They had overcome Ziklag and burned it with fire and taken captive the women and all who were in it, both small and great. They killed no one, but carried them off and went their way. And when David and his men came to the city, they found it burned with fire, and their wives and sons and daughters taken captive. Then David and the people who were with him raised*

their voices and wept until they had no more strength to weep. [129]

However, as David weeps along with his men, he hardly has time enough to dry his tears before they start blaming him for what has happened. They want to stone him. But wait! These are the very same people who God promised that one day he would rule over as king. In fact, David's experience here at Ziklag comes some fifteen years after Samuel anointed him to be the next king of Israel—fifteen years later! David is still *not* king, and now the people have turned against him at Ziklag!

As we wait on the fulfillment of the very call that God has placed on our lives, each of us can expect to come to a place called Ziklag. It is here that we must dig deep and learn to encourage ourselves even though it seems that everything is conspiring to have us abandon the wait.

The Lowest Point in the Journey

Ziklag represents some of the darkest points in our lives. This is the place where it seems that if anything can go wrong it will. Have you been so broken down by a life challenge that you have been weeping and weeping until you cannot weep anymore? You think that this has to be the "bottom of the barrel." There is just no way that things can get any worse, but they do. Ziklag! Ziklag is a place in your life where you might feel most like giving up—no more waiting! Why is it so hard? Why is my situation so difficult?

I remember when I was dating Mark, through the ups and downs of waiting, I shared my experience with a friend, and she told me, "If God is in it, it won't be this hard!" Let me tell you something that I have learned. Sometimes, when God is in it, that is when it gets hard! God is not trying to make it difficult for you. He is good, but the Enemy wants to discourage you the most just before your waiting is almost over. This is the place where you will be most tempted to give up.

The story of Job illustrates well the underlying battle that all believers in Christ face. The Enemy will allow every kind of calamity to befall you with the hopes that you will choose to "curse God and die!"[130] The Devil wants you to doubt God's call on your life. He wants you to quit just before you get your blessing. He wants you to walk out on the story before the grand ending, so he brings you to a low point in your journey. For David, it was Ziklag, for Joseph it was a prison cell, for Jacob it was midnight beside a river, and for Jesus it was in the Garden of Gethsemane.

I don't know what it is for you, but eventually in spite of all the challenges we have already overcome, we come to a place called Ziklag. It is in the place where you are closest to walking into God's calling on your life that you are most vulnerable to walking out and missing the end of the story.

Encouraging Yourself in the Lord

When David returns to camp and sees the destruction that has taken place, he becomes discouraged. Indeed, brook experiences can be times of great discouragement. And unfortunately, they are not a one-time event in the life of a Christian. In fact, as mentioned before, waiting patterns do not happen in a linear fashion nor are the emotions and actions we engage in as we go through these experiences. Sometimes, we overcome one challenge only to end up in another challenging situation even as we are moving forward on our journey. While we can rely on others and our community of faith to be a support around us, ultimately the entire brook experience is a personal one. To obtain the strength we need to make it through the experience and to come out on the other side, we need to pull aside from the crowd and gain our strength and confidence from God.

When I think of David at Ziklag, I have an image of him doing just that. In verse 6 of 1 Samuel 30 we read, *"But David encouraged himself in the Lord his God."* In other translations, *"David strengthened himself in the Lord his God."* Did you notice what is not recorded here? We do not read that David waited on the priest to hold a revival meeting, or David waited for a week of prayer or a retreat to strengthen himself. We do not read that David went to the elders to ask them to pray for him. What is recorded is that *he* (David) encouraged, *himself* (David), in the Lord *his* (David) God. Hallelujah!

I imagine David going off by himself. I see him sitting in the dust with tears running down his face. He is praying and singing quietly, and then louder and louder as he gets strength and encouragement from God. Do you see him repeating the words of some of the very Psalms he penned? I hear him saying:

> *"I lift up my eyes to the mountains—where does my help come from? My help comes from the Lord, the Maker of heaven and earth.*[131]

> *"Yeah though, I walk through the valley of the shadow of death, I will fear no evil for you are with me, Your rod and your staff they comfort me."*[132]

> *"A thousand shall fall at my side and ten thousand at my right hand but they shall not come near me."*[133]

> *"I will bless the Lord at all times, His praise shall continually be in my mouth."*[134]

David spends this time before the Lord getting his strength restored and his faith renewed. Then he goes to God to find out what his next move should be: *"and David inquired of the LORD, "Shall I pursue this raiding party? Will I overtake them?" "Pursue them," he answered. "You will certainly overtake them and succeed in the rescue."*[135] David and his armies go after the Amalekites and deliver such a whooping over them that the Amalekites are not mentioned as an opponent of Israel for many more years. David's men recover every one of their wives and children unharmed, and they recover all that was stolen from them and more. Amazing! David's ability to strengthen himself in the

Lord allows him to persist through the challenges and win.

But if you think that is the end of the story, it is not. The best part is still to come. David and his troops and their families return to Ziklag. And on the third day after his return, a young soldier comes to him and brings news. Saul is dead, and he says, "*I took the crown that was on his head and the bracelet on his arm and have brought them here to my lord.*"[136]

David gets the crown at Ziklag! The crown that he was promised at the age of fifteen comes to him at Ziklag—the place where he has been most distressed, and at one of the lowest points in his journey waiting on God to fulfill the promise to him. This place where he is probably most tempted to give up. It is often in the very places of our deepest distress that if we wait on God patiently, He will bless us. He will fulfill what He has promised to us.

Time with God

To be able to encourage ourselves in the Lord, we must become familiar with His word. That will require us to spend private time with Him. The apostle Paul advises us to pray unceasingly. Some might interpret that to mean that if we are always praying, then we are all set; there is no need for a special devoted time for God where we are free from distractions. That is not the case.

Yes, we are expected to remain in continual communion with God. It is like breathing. We do not need to be reminded to breathe. At the same time, like any relationship that we value, we should also set aside quality time to meet with our Maker and King. It is in these moments as we go through the highs and lows of life that our relationship with God deepens—this is the quintessential image of waiting on Him. When we face life's most difficult challenges, God longs to draw close to us and to strengthen us for the journey. What we need to do is to position ourselves before Him so that we can be strengthened by His personal presence.

At Ziklag we see David taking personal ownership for seeking encouragement from God. His actions illustrate well the difference between personal and communal worship. The Christian journey requires us to exercise many disciplines of our faith. In the book *Spiritual Disciplines for the Christian Life*, Donald S. Whitney defines spiritual disciplines as "those practices found in Scripture that promote spiritual growth among believers in the gospel of Jesus Christ."[137] He identifies two types of disciplines of our faith—private and corporate. Both are needed for us to enter into a deeper relationship with God.

We enjoy the communal disciplines—the coming together of believers to worship, study the word, do ministry, and to encourage each other along the Christian journey. Being in fellowship with like-minded individuals helps us to meet our social-emotional needs. Friends and members can also offer comforting words to us in difficult times. Yes, being in community is encouraging and inspiring. However, even more important than fellowship in community are the personal disciplines that strengthen our relationship with God. The two most important of these are spending time alone in God's word and talking with Him in prayer.

I am inspired when I read the Gospels and see that as much as Jesus was surrounded by large crowds during much of the period of His active ministry, He cultivated the habit of having alone time with His Father. For example, we read the following in the Gospels:

> "But Jesus often withdrew to lonely places and prayed."[138]

> "Early in the morning, while it was still dark, Jesus got up and slipped out to a solitary place to pray."[139]

> "After he had dismissed them, he went up on a mountainside by himself to pray. Later that night, he was there alone."[140]

I imagine that these were the times when Jesus would obtain the strength that He needed from God for the many tasks that He would face in a given day. These were times when He would encourage Himself in His father, God.

Private moments with God are just as important for us. First, it is these time investments that are critical for us to develop a deeper level of intimacy with God. I suggest that it is for this very reason that the Enemy tries to get us so distracted with busyness and "important" stuff in our lives that we often let go of this essential component for Christian growth. Like Martha, we are often so busy doing *important* work, that we fail to do the one thing that is *necessary*—sitting at the feet of Jesus.[141]

When we discipline ourselves to spend one-on-one time with God, we can begin to build up a reservoir of encouragement that will be needed for life challenges up ahead. Even if we are not able to draw aside to a place of solitude in the moment of challenge, we should have already stored up reserves of spiritual comfort from spending time with God that can sustain us when we are at our lowest points. We begin digging the proverbial well before we are thirsty.

An Intimate Relationship

Brook experiences challenge us in myriad ways, but they also provide opportunities for us to slow down, opportunities for us to refocus our lives around the most important elements of the Christian experience, deepening our personal connection with our Maker. When I picture Elijah waiting by the brook, I see a man communing in solitude with his God. Here, he is able to lay aside distractions that get in the way of a deep relational connection with God.

God wants us to take our place in the corporate body of Christ, but He also wants to establish an intimate relationship with each of us. He says: *"before I formed you in the womb I knew you, before you were born I set you apart."*[142] In Luke, we read that *"even the hairs of your head are all numbered."*[143] In 2 Corinthians,

He calls us *"sons and daughters."*[144] We are His children, and He wants to relate to us personally.

I have two daughters and I have learned that one of the duties of a parent is to study each child. My girls are very different. As parents, Mark and I are learning how to be sensitive to their differing needs. In addition to family time, we make time to spend with them individually. It is especially in times of grief or challenge that I need to customize my interaction with each girl. My younger daughter is a talker and a hugger, so what she often needs is to be able to emote and get a comforting hug. My older daughter needs to talk while she is active. Sometimes, we work on a project and talk. Other times, I go up to her room at night time and talk with her as she is reflecting on her day.

In the same way, as children of God, each of us needs to create daily rituals around personal time with our Father. This should be a lifestyle practice where we are consistently and intentionally creating room in our lives to deepen our relationship with Him. The beautiful thing is that even if this has not been your practice in the past, you can start right now to cultivate the habit of finding your encouragement in the Lord your God.

∞∞∞

When we discipline ourselves to spend one-on-one time with God, we can begin to build up a reservoir of encouragement that will be needed for life challenges up ahead.

Chapter 11. Step 6: Persist in the Face of Challenges

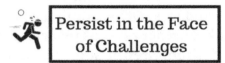 Persist in the Face of Challenges

A Persistent Woman

We do not even know her name. Her identity is buried in the thing that most afflicts her—her suffering. She is known simply as the woman with the *issue of blood*.[145] This is how we come to know her through three separate accounts of her encounter with Jesus as recorded in Matthew, Mark and Luke.[146] Yet if you have suffered long with a private *issue* which is both embarrassing and humbling, her character and her story touches you in a personal way. She has a life challenge that no one wants to talk about. It is the kind of matter that people often speak about in hushed tones—she is constantly bleeding.

I imagine that in her small village people whisper about her when she passes by. They have heard about her condition which in Jewish culture marks her as unclean. As if the physical discomfort and anxiety of her issue is not enough, she also has to deal with the stigma and social isolation that accompanies it. According to Levitical laws, her bleeding makes her unfit for marriage[147] and from religious life[148] as well. Based on these same laws about ritual purity, she is not even fit to be in public.

As is expected for women during menstruation, she should be at home—isolated. Pastor Al Woods of Homewords Ministry describes her situation this way:

> The woman with prolonged menstruation suffered for 12 years from being ritually unclean. This meant she was unable to live a normal life, and was in a sense dead to the people around her. She could not go out, she could not touch members of her family, she could not enjoy a normal life, and she was constantly debilitated.[149]

She has been to see many doctors. She has spent almost all her money in search of a treatment, but still she is without a cure. For twelve years she has borne the shame of her condition. For twelve years she has been suffering. Twelve years is a long time to be waiting for healing. What has she lost during this time? Has she been petitioning God all these years for the cure?

But then she hears about Jesus and the miracles He has been working in the villages around her. Maybe she inquired from those around her about Him. Was it true? Did He really heal the sick? Had he really made the lame walk? A tenuous hope begins arising within her. Perhaps, the Master can heal her too. Perhaps, but .... It would require action on her part—desperate action.

She is not going to stay at home and hope that Jesus will pass by. She will not only kneel on the floor in the safety of her room and pray for healing. No! She will also act on her faith; she will make her way to Jesus. So, she begins planning and preparing for her encounter with the Master. She will first need to find out the expected route that Jesus will be traveling and make her way there. Yes! That is what she will do! No longer will she sit in her suffering hoping for the cure. She will make her way to Jesus and put herself on the path for His blessings.

But when she gets there, positioned on the path for her healing, the crowd is too thick. It might be that she begins to doubt for a moment that she will be able to make it through this crowd. Will people recognize and shun her? She lingers for a moment, but she remains resolute. She has come too far to turn back now. Somehow, she manages to make her way through the crowd. She is persistent. Can you see her pushing through that crowd of people all with urgent needs as well? She is determined. She gets within arm's length of the Master's robe, and she stretches out her hand and touches the hem of His garment. And *"immediately her bleeding stopped."*[150]

She took initiative.

She acted on her faith, and through her persistent effort she was healed.

Obstacle After Obstacle

Expect to be challenged while you wait by the brook. In fact, life has a way of putting obstacle after obstacle in our paths the closer we get to our destination. It is at these times that we may be most tempted to abandon the journey—to give up on God.

If there is one quality that stands out in the story of the woman with the issue of blood, it is this: she was persistent. She was determined to do what it took to get to the other side of her waiting experience. Her determination was such that she could not and would not sit idly by and wait. Instead, she took advantage of every opportunity to seek remedy after remedy, and she did not stop until she was healed. She went from one doctor to the next until her money was just about used up. I wonder how many times she had sat in a proverbial waiting room, hoping and praying that this would be the day that she would get the cure for her affliction. How many times had she tried home brewed remedies suggested to her by well-meaning relatives or family friends? Drink this. Eat this. Brew that. Over the course of twelve years nothing had worked. How many days and nights had she wrestled with God pouring out her heart to Him late into the night and even into the wee hours of the morning? Was she on the verge of giving up, of losing all hope?

Finally, when she hears about Jesus, hope awakens again. But even in her attempt to secure her healing from Jesus, other obstacles present themselves. She must venture into the crowd and risk the shame and stigma of her condition being found out. The crowd is also so dense that she is not sure that she will get through or even be able to have a word with Jesus. It may be that she thought about turning back—about abandoning her mission. What if she had? If she had, she would have been one touch away from her healing but still missing out.

There is a true and infamous story of a man by the name of R. U. Hardy. During the time of the gold fever in America, he and his uncle set out for Colorado and staked a claim for a gold mine. The work was difficult but they kept at it and eventually hit a gold vein. They were ecstatic, so they raised money to get the machinery to continue to retrieve the gold out of the mine, and continued digging, looking and hoping for the big pay day. But as they dug and dug day after day, nothing happened. Finally, they gave up and sold the machinery to a junk dealer.

But the junk dealer was curious about the potential of the mine, so he decided to find out exactly what the problem was. The junk dealer had an engineer come out to assess the situation. Here's the shocker! The engineer found that just three feet away from where Harby and his uncle had stopped drilling was where the gold vein was located. Just three more feet of drilling from where his predecessors had stopped, the junk dealer found gold! This story illustrates beautifully the observation made by the English theologian and historian, Thomas Fuller, "It is always darkest just before the Day dawneth."[151]

Whenever I read the story of Jesus and His last night of ministry on this earth, I see that pattern of increased challenge and frustration just before Jesus completes the mission that He has been assigned. Jesus has been with His disciples for three years, teaching them about the kingdom of heaven, about how to love one another and how to serve one another. Still on the very night that He is going to begin the final chapter of His earthly ministry, it would appear as though all the lessons He has been attempting to teach them have been in vain. The disciples have not learned the principles of servant leadership. They end up quibbling about who should wash each other's feet. Judas goes out that very night to betray Him, and when Jesus asks the disciples to pray with Him on the night when they should have known what was ahead, they are asleep.[152]

It would seem like it is the opportune time for Jesus to recognize that maybe these people are not worth the price He has to pay to redeem them. Yet, in spite of His suffering, at this point in His ministry when He is tempted to abandon the mission, He does not. He goes on to fulfill His Father's calling on His life. He prays: *"Nevertheless, not my will but thy will be done."*[153]

Persisting in the Face of Challenges

To persist in the face of challenges is to continue to believe God's calling on your life and to advance forward even when the outcome remains uncertain. However, what often happens to us as we wait on God is that we begin to doubt God's plan for our lives. We may even begin to doubt our abilities to succeed. If God has promised us, as He did for Joseph, that He will accomplish a great work in our life, and we find ourselves facing delay after delay, the Devil moves in quickly to attack our confidence:

> *"There is no way you can be a doctor, that is too hard!"*

> *"Do you really think you have what it takes to start your own business? You don't know the first thing about money!"*

> *"You are not really that good at teaching, preaching and leading."*

> *"You know you can't write, or cook, or sing, or play the piano, or sew or clean etc., etc."*

Does it sound familiar? You will remember that when God called Moses to go to Pharaoh on behalf of the children of Israel, Moses replied: *"Who me?. . . O Lord, I'm not very good with words.*

I never have been, and I'm not now, even though you have spoken to me. I get tongue-tied, and my words get tangled."[154] When Moses does eventually go, Pharaoh does not listen the first time, nor the second time nor the third time. It takes ten plagues for Pharaoh to agree to let the children of Israel go, and even then, Pharaoh still continues to pursue them up to the point of the Red Sea.[155]

We must come to the point in our brook experiences where we are willing to go forward with the mission regardless of what obstacles are thrown in our path. We go forward because God has a call on our life. Persistence for the widow meant taking step after step towards her healing and deliverance. Persistence for this woman meant continuing to believe that her healing was to be found in her relentless pursuit of God.

When Persisting Means Giving Up

There is also a more critical aspect of persistence that is necessary for us to adopt to make it through our brook experiences successfully. Yes, we must come to the place as this widow did where we accept that the answers that we seek for whatever the ailment is only found in the person of Jesus Christ. However, that acceptance is only the first step in this act of persistence.

The real test of our maturing faith walk with God is our willingness to persist in our *relationship with* Him even if He chooses not to heal us. You see, the issue is not the bleeding after all. The real issue is our need for healing of the relational breach between us and God. Are we prepared to do what it takes to experience that kind of healing? Will we persist even if God chooses to allow us to wait longer than expected for the answers we seek, and even if He continues to keep from us the thing we most desire? Will we persist even if the bleeding does not stop? That is the real test!

In this second step in the act of persisting, we may be required to let go of the very thing we so desperately want rather than have it stand in the way of deeper intimacy with God. This was the kind of persistence that Job showed even after he lost everything. Satan's accusation was that Job was only serving God because He was blessing him by giving him win after win without losses. *"Remove his blessings,"* the deceiver suggested, *"and Job will curse you!"*[156] So, God allowed Satan to inflict on Job one of the most trying of brook experiences recorded in the Bible, but Job held firm and still clung to his relationship with God in spite of the circumstances in which he found himself. He said, *"Though he slay me, yet will I trust in him."*[157] He continued to bless God even after he faced loss after loss, even after he faced discouragement from those around him—his closest friends and even His own wife. Rather than blaming God or listening to the counsel of those around him, Job relied on and leaned into his relationship with God to sustain him through this difficult time. He was willing to lose everything but his relationship with God.

This is a lesson that I had to learn during the time Mark and I were dating. After we met in the summer of 2000 in response to answered prayers, you would think that the path to marriage was easy for us. It was not. Mark and I dated for six years. Yes, you heard that right! Six years! We had to work through major relational issues. The time of waiting was a frustrating period for us, and especially for me. I felt my biological clock which had been quietly ticking before we met, growing louder and louder into an annoying crescendo. After almost six years of dating, I finally decided to walk out—but not on God. I decided to walk out on the confidence I had placed in the notion that my future was bound up with Mark. It was not! It was bound up with God, and His will and timing for my life.

Somewhere along our dating path without even realizing it, I had thought it best to take matters into my own hands. I was not trusting God and His timing for us. The most worrisome thing was that I had not surrendered my desire for a lifelong mate fully to Him. What led to my breakthrough is perhaps not intuitive. Please don't miss this point. Persisting with God often requires us to give up something else. I had to give up hopes for married life to be found in Mark, and trust that if God had brought Mark to me, He could bring someone else to me as well. I would persist in finding my answer in God and not in the person He had sent me. Once I made that decision, I was in a place of alignment with God's will for my life. It was a painful surrender, but it was also a very liberating one.

I still remember the day that I called "Mom" to tell her that Mark and I had reached an impasse in our relationship. I was crying and she was crying—after so many years of dating, we were family. I told her that she had raised a wonderful son and I could not say anything bad about him—he was a good man. But things just were not working out for us towards a happily ever after. I told her I was going to go on and trust that God would take care of me and that He would also take care of Mark on the road ahead of us. It was shortly after I made the decision to walk out of this relationship and to trust God for the next one, that Mark proposed.

The Relationship is the Thing

The story of this nameless woman with the issue of blood is as much about persistence as it is about surrender. Her singular focus on having a healing encounter with Jesus meant that she had to be willing to let go of the hope that her healing would come from the doctors with whom she had already spent so much of her life savings. She had to let go of her persistence in the direction of manmade efforts and redirect her persistence towards her faith walk. She had to persist in her determination to meet with Jesus.

However, persisting in the face of challenges is also about learning to put the pursuit of God over the pursuit of the things we want. Here's why. If we are not attentive to the relational aspect of the brook experience, we run the risk of using our time there to our detriment. Something tragic can happen to us as we wait that can derail us on the path to mission fulfillment—

we can end up making the object of the waiting an idol itself. We begin to value it more than the relationship with God. As important as our purpose is, or our healing, our breakthrough, a marriage proposal, the birth of a child etc.—we ultimately lose if we make that more valuable than the gift of greater intimacy with God. In this instance, persistence in the face of challenges comes to us when we are prepared to surrender the thing we most want in life to God and to trust Him for the rest of the journey. Even if he does not heal us, even if the baby dies, even if "the thorn in the flesh" remains, we will not give up on the relationship with God!

Persisting in the face of challenges is about persevering in our relationship with God while we wait. It may even require us to give up on the very thing we desire—to choose to let it go and still continue in our pursuit of the God of the wait.

To persist in the face of challenges is to continue to believe God's calling on your life and to advance forward even when the outcome remains uncertain.

Chapter 12. Step 7: Profit from the Pain

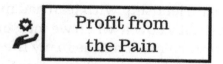

Comforting a Friend

In the summer of 2009, I sat in the living room at the home of my friend, Jean. She had been battling lymphoma for five years with chemotherapy, blood transfusions, regular visits to the doctor's office, and hospital stays. I was meeting with her on the eve of her hospital stay for a stem cell surgery. This surgery had the potential to replace all her cancerous cells with healthy new cells harvested from her sister. It was a big step, and there were tremendous risks. We were concerned that she might survive the surgery, but that her body would reject the new cells and be compromised by graft versus host disease.[158] However, this scheduled surgery was the best hope for a viable life without the regular rounds of chemotherapy and all of the attendant side effects that had plagued her days for the last several years.

In the weeks and months leading up to this evening, Jean and I had questioned our way through many conversations. She struggled with the "Why me?" and the "Why now?" questions. For much of her adult life she had been a stay-at-home mom to two children while supporting her husband, who worked in the area of higher education. When the children were a little older, she began going to school part-time in the afternoon after her husband returned from work. Bit by bit she was able to complete her bachelor's degree, then her master's degree, and finally she had gone on to earn a doctorate in 2004. That same year, she had been able to secure her first tenure track position as an assistant professor. On the brink of this new phase in her life journey, she was diagnosed with lymphoma.

On this summer afternoon as we stood with the weight of the hopes and risks of this major surgery bearing down on us, I reflected on what friendship with Jean had meant to me over the years. Jean did not know it when we met, but the gift of her friendship had come to me at a time in my life when I was very much in need of a friend. She was the answer that had come out of one of my own brook experiences. For years, I had been asking God to lead me to an old-fashioned kind of friendship—not the Facebook kind of friendship that can be as substantive as vapor, but the kind of friendship that is as deep and hearty as a warm bowl of split pea soup on a cold winter's night. By the time I met Jean, I had already lived in three countries. Having uprooted myself so many times, quite a few of my previous sister-to-sister friendships had suffered through the challenge of distance and time. Without a doubt, I knew that in answer to my prayers God had sent Jean to me.

She and I met towards the end of the summer of 2004. We were both freshly minted PhDs and new hires in the College of Education at my current university. Her office was right next to mine, and without preamble our friendship developed. She was a kindred spirit. Together we navigated the challenges of university culture as newbies. Through our collective struggles and joys our friendship deepened.

Jean had a special gift for friendship. She cultivated it as an art by practicing sacrificial kindnesses. At the time that we met, Mark and I had already been dating four years, and Jean became my confidant through some of challenges he and I experienced in those years. Jean was the one to whom I confessed that I was tired of waiting for him to propose. When she finally met him, she "ooohed" and "ahhhed" about how handsome he was. "Oh Kathy," she said. "It's going to happen soon. Just wait." Her joy could barely be contained when she saw the ring; we hugged each other and cheered.

As only God could orchestrate, Jean was also with me in some of the most significant moments of my life. She was the only person in the office with me late on the Friday afternoon when I got the sad news that my father had passed away. She held me close as I cried. In the days and weeks that followed, she found thoughtful ways to encircle me with the comforting presence of a caring friend—lunch dates at our favorite spots, a thoughtful card, and the gift of a hand-painted cross with a verse from my favorite psalm—Psalm 27. On my wedding day, she and her husband were the first persons I saw when I arrived at the church. Our eyes met, and her radiant face beamed with joy. There was no need for words.

One of my most cherished memories of her is when she showed up at my door for my first baby shower. In spite of undergoing a taxing round of drug therapy a few days before, I opened the door, and there she was. When I saw her, she looked pale and weak, but she said simply, "I could not miss it for anything." Then when the baby did arrive, she made a beeline for our house to greet our daughter Alyssa and shower her with more gifts. Yes, my friendship with Jean was a rare and beautiful thing.

But on this day in early summer, I felt the weight of the questions "Why me?" Why now?" bearing down on us both. I was asking myself those same questions. The thought of losing this once in a lifetime kind of friendship pressed heavily on my heart. But I did not speak of that.

I spoke about something else. Throughout our friendship, we had spoken in bits and spurts about my own "why me?" experiences. But as we stood there on that day, I suddenly saw, with a clarity that had escaped me for many years, that all the pain, hurt, and abuse I had experienced in my early life, had prepared me in a unique way for this very moment. From a place where I had tried to bury much of the pain of my early years, I reached down deep and pulled out my "bruised and bloodied heart"[159]. I shared with Jean in detail and with anguish, stories of rejection, hurt and marginalization—and the times I had cried out to God to ask "Why me"? But I did not stop there. I continued to show her how each of those experiences had prepared me to be the woman she was talking to at that very moment —I hoped a compassionate friend, who had risen from humble beginnings—the least likely to succeed, and the first in her immediate family to earn a doctoral degree, a mother of a one year old at the time—who could empathize with her experience and could say to her with great conviction, "Jean, there is power in this experience."

And in that moment, I was so very grateful for the pain of my many waiting experiences because they had been preparing me for this very occasion—to comfort my dear friend. I saw clearly that my heavenly *"Father of compassion and the God of all comfort, who comforts us in all our troubles,"* had allowed me to wait by my brooks *"so that [I]could comfort those in any trouble with the comfort [I had received] from God"*.[160]

There is a cost attached to the losses we experience as we wait beside the brook. That cost is pain. However, we can choose to allow that pain to cripple us or we can come to accept it as one of the most valuable tools in our ministry. We can choose to profit from the pain.

Profiting from the Pain

Jean died later that summer. Shortly after we met in her living room on the eve of her hospital stay, I left Philadelphia to attend a month-long program at the University of Michigan. Just a few weeks later, almost five years after my father had passed, I found myself on another plane headed back to Philadelphia weeping for the loss of a dear friend. I grieved the loss of Jean, and truthfully there are not many days that go by even now that

I do not stop and think of her and my eyes tear up. I still miss my friend.

However, my experience with Jean showed me convincingly that our most difficult life experiences, as painful as they may be, are the very experiences that uniquely qualify us for ministry to others. Growing up as a child who was abandoned by a mother was difficult, and I could choose to focus on the pain of that experience. In fact, for much of my early years, I did do just that. It was necessary for me to grieve the loss in its entirety and to acknowledge the ways in which this experience had real impacts on my developing identity. Through the years, I was able to process the grief and the pain by seeking help from professional counselors and spiritual advisors. For those of us who have had traumatizing life events seeking help is indeed important and necessary. There is no need to spiritualize that for which we can find practical solutions. Yes, we should pray about it, but then we should also do everything possible to avail ourselves of the resources that God continues to provide for our help and healing.

But after we have processed our grief, we do have a choice to make. Moreover, this is not a "one and done" decision; this is a choice that we will be confronted with again and again as we face each new life challenge. Are we going to allow the bad things that happen to us to define us or are we going to use them to strengthen us so we can continue to advance towards our God given purpose? As I have stood at many major crossroads in my life, I have found that this question continues to present itself to me. Yet at every turn it has been a difficult choice because I have been tested at increasing levels of difficulty. However, as I continue to challenge myself to move forward in spite of the blows that are leveled at me through this journey of life, it becomes easier with each encounter to make the decision because I know the direction in which I am headed. Yes! I choose to advance in spite of the circumstance!

As we learn to wait on God and to trust Him for our journey, we become empowered to use our most challenging brook experiences to do a massive revision of the script. We develop the ability to rewrite the narrative of defeat into a narrative of triumph.

So what story are you writing? As I have studied the biographies of many iconic individuals who made significant contributions in life, I have been encouraged to see that the genesis of their life work was often birthed in moments of great pain "Why me?" moments!

A girl born in St. Louis in 1928 is abused at the age of eight and becomes mute in the wake of this tragedy, rarely opening her mouth to speak for several years. At the age of seventeen, she becomes a single parent. This same young woman grows up to become one of the foremost icons of American poetry, prose and thought. Say the name—Maya Angelou![161]

A man is arrested, and convicted of committing sabotage against South Africa's government in a fight against the evil system of apartheid, and spends twenty-seven years in prison. After being released from prison, he becomes South Africa's first Black president in 1994. Say the name—Nelson Mandela![162]

A young girl is struck by a disease that leaves her deaf, blind and mute. Undaunted, that woman goes on to become one of the twentieth century's leading humanitarians advocating on behalf of others living with disabilities, and helping to found the American Civil Liberties Union. Say the name—Helen Keller![163]

These individuals all navigated challenging moments in life —moments when they probably felt most alone and lacked clarity about next steps. Even though our experiences may pale in comparison to theirs, our own brook experiences in the context of our relationship with God challenge us too in ways that are unique to our circumstances.

However, what if instead of viewing these experiences as weaknesses, we learned to embrace them as gifts? What if we harnessed the power within them to ignite our passions to find our path to meaningfully serve and comfort others?

The Gifts of Adversity

I have not always thought of my brook experiences as beneficial, useful, or wonderful resources in my cache of tools that could propel me onward to accomplishing my life purpose. What? Abandonment by my mother? Beneficial? Useful? You've got to be kidding me! Abandonment, abuse, rejection, terminal illness—these are not good. How can we come to accept such experiences as gifts?

Andrew Solomon, a professor of psychology at Columbia University, in a TED talk entitled "How the worst moments in our lives make us who we are"[164] recounted an experience that occurred while he was conducting interviews for his book *Far from the Tree*.[165] In this book, he narrates the experiences of families dealing with children who are different, and the quest to make meaning of it all. One mother he interviewed who had two children with severe multiple disabilities said: "Children like ours are not pre-ordained as gifts; they are a gift because that is what we have chosen."

Each of us has the capacity with God's help whenever we make it to the other side of one brook experience or as we continue to navigate through a seemingly endless, never ending brook experience to make that choice every day—to accept our brook experience as a gift.

To use an analogy from the business world, we can make a choice to *profit from the pain* of our experiences. A profit is defined as "the financial benefit realized when revenue generated from a business activity exceeds the expenses."[166] To profit from our brook experiences is to choose to change how we think about these experiences. In the process of embracing the action steps of waiting (*grieving our loss, wrestling with God, pivoting to praise, developing in darkness, encouraging ourselves in the Lord, and persisting in the face of challenges*), something wonderful can happen to us. We can arrive at the place where we are able to view what happened to us as a "life advantage" or "life benefit" that uniquely qualifies us to help others facing their own brook experiences.

This is exactly what God has been preparing you to be able to do. This is what God has been preparing me to do as I have been waiting by the brook. From a very practical perspective, to profit from the pain is to do what Andrew Solomon recommends—we can "forge meaning" from our brook experiences.

Connecting the Broken Pieces

One of the biggest tasks each of us faces on the road to personal fulfillment and meaningful service is to connect the broken places of our lives to our calling. In the book *Finding Calcutta*, Mary Poplin, a professor of education and a regular presenter on the influence and legacy of Mother Teresa's life, recounts how two months that she spent working alongside Mother Teresa caring for the crippled, the abandoned and the dying in the streets of India taught her important lessons about meaningful work and service. Poplin writes:

> Often people teach that to know our calling, we must know our spiritual gifts, desires, opportunities and special skills. Clearly, these are all useful. However, it is perhaps even more that our crises and grieving reveal our call.[167]

The biographies of so many men and women provide evidence of the truth of this observation that it is often our most painful experiences that reveal to us what we are called to do.

Sometime ago I heard the story about the experiences of Katherine Wolf. At the age of twenty-six, this new mother of a six-month-old son suffered a massive brain stem stroke that almost killed her. The stroke ended her promising modeling career and changed her life drastically. Through the physical pain of her injuries and the mental anguish that accompanied her questionings to God, Katherine and her husband Jay chose to make the paradigm shift in thinking that allows them to be able to *profit from the pain* of that tragic experience.

The couple founded a non-profit ministry, "Hope Heals," with a mission to reach out to people with broken brains, broken hearts, broken stories—people that are broken.[168] They have also co-authored two books: "*Hope Heals*,"[169] which offers a detailed account of Katherine's near death experience; and "*Suffer Strong*,"[170] in which they challenge readers to embrace suffering as a privilege, rather than a punishment—to recognize that "suffering isn't the end of your story; it's the beginning of a new story."[171]

Even though Katherine continues to deal with chronic pain and loss of mobility as a result of her injury, she is choosing to suffer in strength rather than in weakness. When asked how she is able to continue to deal with this life challenge, Katherine says she has learned to intentionally cultivate joy that can sustain her—to recognize that what she "knows to be true of God in the light is still true of Him in the dark".[172] She says, "I don't hate the darkness. . . This darkness is doing something very powerful in me. I will emerge differently from what I am going through. There is treasure in this darkness. God is doing something in you in a season of deep darkness."[173]

Writing this book has allowed me to retrace the losses I have experienced so far in my life, sometimes with tears in my eyes, but more often than not with a sense of gratitude. I thought about the abuse at the hands of stepmothers, the loss of my dad at a time in my life when I should have been celebrating with him, the many years I spent growing up with low-self-esteem thinking that I was not worthy to be loved if my own mother had rejected me. I thought of the struggles I experienced to pursue higher education, how hard I worked to be able to pay my bills as a graduate student, eating rice and beans for days because they were the least expensive items on the menu. I thought about waiting and waiting for the man who would become my husband, even while I made mistake after mistake when I tried to choose on my own. I thought about the most recent long brook experience with the job search to be a senior administrator at the university only for the door to close in my face as I was about to walk through it. I also thought about the death of my friend, Jean. These are all important chapters of my life story. However, to overemphasize those aspects of the narrative would be to slight "the precious gift" of these experiences. Yes, "a gift!"

I am convinced now more than ever before that my many brook experiences and crises were the very things I needed to go through to be able to write this book from a place of deep compassion and understanding. It is from this personal space that I can connect with you and offer you some "comfort" as you go through your own trying experiences.

Whatever your brook experiences are, they will certainly be challenging. You will experience pain and even suffering. But know this! The experiences that you are having in your moments of darkness are qualifying you to be able to minister to others facing their own seasons of waiting. These experiences are also preparing you to fulfill God's great purpose for your life — beside the brook is the ideal spot for you to receive custom made gifts from God that have your name written on them.

∞∞∞

One of the biggest tasks each of us faces on the road to personal fulfillment and meaningful service is to connect the broken places of our lives to our calling.

Chapter 13. The Gifts of Waiting

Valuing What Matters Most

In 2008 Mark and I came to a fork in the road along our life path. At the time, I was deep into my scholarship as a tenure track professor but feeling the strain of everything I was trying to accomplish now as a professor, wife, mother, and part-time consultant. Likewise, Mark was doing extremely well as a financial consultant at one of the top four US consulting firms. He was in line to be a partner and busier than ever. The vision of professional success and financial stability lured us forward. But for several years even before this time, we had found ourselves reassessing the cost of it all.

When we were dating, Mark sat me down at his dining table one night and showed me his three-year plan for making partner. In the years that followed, he had done the work to make this happen. We had committed his efforts to God. But at every turn, Mark found his head hitting the concrete ceiling.[174] In the last one hundred years in the history of his firm only one other Black person had made it to partner in our state. Undaunted, however, he persisted. Then early in 2008, we could see things lining up for him to hit the numbers with millions of dollars in business brought into the firm, and surpassing his previous sales record. Maybe this would be the year that he would make it. God would finally answer our prayers! We would finally be able to declare ourselves financially free!

Then it happened—the great global financial crisis of 2008. After the crisis, an already brutal sixty plus hour work week became even more demanding—the work pulled him on planes, trains and automobiles here, there, and everywhere. He was gone mostly every week to another city and state. To attain the elusive dream of partnership, he would now have to sacrifice even more of his time.

However, even before the crisis, we had begun rethinking our life path. We were experiencing changes in ourselves and in our family circle. In 2007 our first daughter was born, and then in 2010 we welcomed our second daughter. Now we were more aware of the value of Mark's increasing time investments for the firm, and we felt deeply troubled by the fact that we were not owners of any of these investments.

Mark was also missing out on valuable time with the girls, and I was becoming more and more frazzled as a pseudo-single working parent every week when he was away. Yet in spite of the professional demands on our time, we were convicted by the call of Nehemiah to the families of Israel to *"fight for our families."*[175] through more hands-on Christian parenting. Ultimately, our current life path was proving to be inconsistent with our faith values. We began to question how we could be better stewards of what God had given us. There had to be reasons why God had not allowed the partnership door to open for us. We were now convinced that it was because He was leading us down a different path. That path included visions of a better quality of life–more unhurried family time–and greater progress toward the legacy that our parents had begun. We wanted to leave behind a richer legacy than a company pension plan.

And so in 2014, Mark made the decision to walk away from it all—to quit the firm and begin working for himself from our home. We were going to be owners. However, when Mark told me his decision, panic set in. How were we going to live? We had kids to put through college! What about the risks? The lure of a stable paycheck to which we had set our GPS was tempting —it threatened to cripple our movement forward. Though the vision was clear, the pathway to getting there was murky. We were afraid, but we were going to follow God's lead.

For the next several months and years after that decision, Mark and I weathered the transition as we waited by this brook. We made the necessary and often painful adjustments in our lifestyle and spending habits. It was hard on us both; the anxieties were real. We learned to rely heavily on God to navigate the relational tensions that often erupted between us during this time.

In his private way, I watched Mark grieve the loss of his partnership dream and question his way through this time of uncertainty. Together we wrestled with God about why he had allowed Mark to get so close and no closer, and then given him another game plan altogether. We were also unsure about what lay ahead of us. But in the midst of our doubts, we began to pivot into praise. We learned to encourage ourselves in God's word, and we persisted to the other side of the brook.

Now six years out from that transition, we see clearly the benefits we received out of that decision. We have an even better level of financial stability now than before using the very gifts with which God has blessed us. But more importantly, we are satisfied that we have been able to connect our faith walk with our professional aspirations. We have a deeper level of relational intimacy with God, with each other, and with our children. The inputs of time and intentional parenting that we are investing in our children are yielding the kinds of results for which we continue to pray and hope for. Finally, the kind of fiscal responsibility and attention to Christian stewardship that we learned to practice then were the very things that Mark needed to experience to now help others on their own journey. Mark understands the work that God is positioning Him to do next. These were the gifts that were borne out of our season of adversity.

The Gifts of Waiting on God

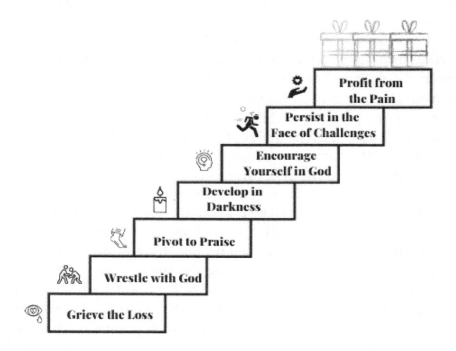

Brook experiences provide us with much needed opportunities to work on the most important curriculum in life—
learning to value what truly matters. The school of adversity
contains the best training rooms for us to begin to see clearly
that our central life focus should not be about the things that
we want most in this life as important as they may be. The most
critical area of focus needs to be on the relationships that we
spend time cultivating: our relationship with God, our relationship with ourselves as broken individuals in need of a Savior,
and our relationships with others. These are the very gifts that
come to us as we learn to wait patiently on God.

Intimacy with God

Intimacy
with God

It is in the waiting spot that we
are positioned to receive the
gift of a more intimate relationship with God. Waiting on God
is as much about *waiting on* Him
to act in the way that we have
prayed as it is about waiting
with Him. If we can focus on the
"*waiting with Him*" part of the
dynamic, more than the "*waiting on Him*" to do what we have
asked part, we can allow ourselves to be enveloped in the
beauty of a deepening relationship with our Father. This deepening relationship is the real
gift of the wait. It is a gift that
remains with us long after the outcome of our prayers have been
realized, or even if we do not get the outcome for which we are
waiting. In fact, one of the biggest tragedies of the Christian experience is for us to become so focused on what we are waiting
for that we fail to fully benefit from a deep relational encounter

with the person with whom we are waiting.

One of the great benefits of brook experiences in cultivating a deeper connection between us and God is that they provide us with a distraction free environment where God has our attention. Beside the brook Cherith, Elijah waited on God in solitude; here, he learned to depend more fully on God for direction and next steps. In the belly of the whale, Jonah was given time to think and recalibrate the direction for his life. Likewise, our own brook experiences position us to look upward.

As believers, our everyday connections to God though consistent can lack relational depth because we have fallen into a routinized kind of pseudo engagement. For example, as a couple, Mark and I are very blessed in that we both get to work from home. We are around each other almost 24-7. There is a natural rhythm to our days that involve greeting each other in the morning, interacting together as a family, and sharing meals together etc. Still, being around each other most of the time does not equate with quality relational inputs. In the same way, in the regular tempo of our daily life we can fall into a spiritual rut where the time we do spend with God lacks a certain depth of effort that is necessary for the relationship to grow. We are not engaging in "gut-level" praying, or hungrily studying the word, or devoutly meditating on the goodness of God. Is it possible that what the Lord has said about His people is also true of us? *"These people come near to me with their mouth and honor me with their lips, but their hearts are far from me. Their worship of me is based on merely human rules they have been taught."*[176]

Ah, but all that changes when we end up by the brook. Our engagement with God takes on greater tenacity when we realize that there is no other solution for us as Larnelle Harris sings, "But God."[177] We have a deeper appreciation of our need for God and to connect with Him. That is when our prayers rise above pretension and we begin to pour out the earnest needs of our heart to God. This is the space where intimacy develops. Here, our "knee-grazing-the-floor-three-minutes-say-the-same-thing-over-and-over again" kinds of prayers just aren't going to cut it! Brook experiences raise our praying life to a new level. As we wrestle with God as Jacob did and as Hannah did, intimacy develops.

This is the kind of praying where you can't stop talking with God. You have so much to tell Him, and the time is too short before you have to head off to work or to the task ahead! These are the kinds of prayers where you get up off your knees with a runny nose and tears running down your cheek because your heart is so full and the emotional connection is so raw. Do you know what I am talking about?

As difficult as it is for us to comprehend or appreciate, sometimes God has to allow us to sit by the brook without the myriad of distractions that crowd out space for Him in our lives so that He can give us one more opportunity to get to know Him better? God is willing to put everything on the line—to go "all in" to save us eternally because He knows that our salvation can only be found in a deep relationship with Him.

Spiritual Transformation

Spiritual Transformation

Through the process of waiting patiently on God our character is also being developed and refined. When we decide to follow Jesus, and we diligently practice the disciplines of our Christian faith, we are gifted with spiritual transformation. As we develop a deeper relationship with God our character begins to more and more resemble His. The apostle Paul likens this perfecting of character to a race. He urges all who call themselves Christians to run the race to WIN!

Do you not know that in a race all the runners run, but only one gets the prize? Run in such a way as to get the prize. Everyone who competes in the games goes into strict training. They do it to get a crown that will not last, but we do it to get a crown that will last forever.[178]

How do Christians train to win? How do we get to practice our faith walk more authentically with each passing day? How do we become better at doing the Christian thing?

Paul offers the following advice to young Timothy. He tells him that he should discipline himself *"for the purpose of godliness."*[179] In the King James Version of the Bible, the last part of this verse reads, *"Exercise thyself rather unto godliness."*—EXERCISE. Did you know that the Greek word for "exercise" here is the same word from which we get the English word "gymnasium" or "gym" for short? This word was only used to describe the professional athletes of that time. When these athletes trained and competed, they had rigorous training schedules. Paul is saying to Timothy, "Do you see how athletes train their bodies for an outcome that is temporary? You must train yourself for an even greater prize."

That advice is for us too. We must discipline ourselves to wait patiently on God by practicing spiritual disciplines of our faith. As discussed previously, spiritual disciplines are practices that promote our spiritual growth. Brook experiences provide the perfect field work setting that allows us to practice the kind of disciplined actions that are necessary for character development.

Here is the amazing thing about our waiting experiences. Enveloped in the seven action steps of waiting by the brook are disciplines of the faith:

Grieving the Loss— prayer, worship, journaling, solitude.

Wrestling with God— prayer, solitude, worship, fasting.

Pivoting to Praise—worship, prayer, solitude.

Developing in Darkness—prayer, stewardship, service, secrecy, frugality, simplicity.

Encouraging Ourselves in God—solitude, silence, Bible study, journaling, personal meditation, fasting.

Persisting in the Face of Challenges —persistence in practicing the disciplines of our faith.

Profiting from the Pain—commitment to ministry and service.

These are the very actions that strengthen our spiritual muscle and allow God to do His transforming work on our character.

As Christians, most of us are well aware of many of these spiritual disciplines of engagement that are necessary for our growth –prayer, Bible study, worship etc. But that is not all that is needed. Waiting on God often requires us to give up certain things that are also necessary for our character development —to practice disciplines of disengagement. In the book *Abundant Simplicity,* Jan Johnson, a well-known writer and speaker on Christian spirituality, writes:

> Christians have mostly practiced disciplines of engagement, such as study, prayer, service, worship and fellowship. Disciplines of abstinence, however, such as fasting, solitude, silence, chastity, secrecy, frugality, and simplicity of speech and item, help us let go of life-draining behaviors. We need to exhale what is unnecessary as well as inhale nourishment from God.[180]

If we really want to experience the spiritual transformation that we seek, it not only requires us to practice disciplines of engagement with God, it also requires us to cultivate habits of disengagement from distractions that dilute the potency of our connection to Him.

Growing up in Trinidad, I remember the early morning wake up calls by my dad to drink a cup of Senna leaves steeped in hot water for the annual "cleaning out," or in local speak, "a purge." For those of you who may not know, Senna is a plant that works as a natural laxative. Okay, so this was definitely not one of my favorite childhood rituals! However, I think this experience is an apt metaphor for habits that support spiritual growth.

In our Christian life it is possible for us to get so bloated with the distractions of life that it actually stunts our spiritual growth. We end up in need of a spiritual purge. Brook experiences provide us with opportunities to not only practice the disciplines of engagement with God, but to also practice disengagement from the minutiae of daily living—the purgative aspect of growth. Both of these components of spiritual disciplines are critical for our spiritual transformation.

A Call to Meaningful Service

Meaningful Service

As we navigate our brook experience, we are also gifted with clarity about the work that God has called us to do next. However, that clarity is often birthed through pain— through struggle.

Most of us would be happy if God would clearly and audibly tell us the purpose that He has for our life. We long for a once and for all burning bush experience like Moses.[181] However, even as there are many instances when God revealed His will directly and audibly to individuals, there are instances where God's will was revealed in different ways. In the book *Whisper*, Mark Batterson writes that "God speaks to different personalities in different ways. The way Jesus related to His disciples was as different as Peter, James and John."[182]

The critical element to understanding God's will for our life is to get to know God personally in the context of an ongoing relational dialogue. A growing adult who has to wait to hear their father's clear, authoritarian directive whenever they are faced with any decision is one who has not matured sufficiently. Maturing adults are able to rely on the wisdom and insights they have been given by their parents through deepening relationships with them to make wise decisions. Similarly, in the context of our relationship with God, we should not expect God to tell us every answer to every life question so that we can respond as robots. Instead, we must learn to rely on Him for guidance in our decision making. Our prayer becomes the prayer of Solomon: *"So give your servant a discerning heart . . . to distinguish between right and wrong."*[183]

It might be comforting to think that there is one thing that God has called us to do during our lifetime, but that is not the case. God calls us to occupy different roles at different times in our lives. The more we choose to get in sync with God's will for our life, the easier it is for us to discern what that role is at various points in our life journey.

As we engage in the seven action steps involved in patiently waiting on God, our paradigm begins to shift. We are able to view each challenge we face differently, understanding it as part of the master design for our lives through which God is leading us. We are able to view each brook experience through new lenses:

It is not an ending, but it is a beginning.

It is not a season of punishment, but it is a season of preparation.

It is not a time for resignation, but it is an opportunity to build new expectations.

It is not a time of helpless dependence, but it is an invitation for alignment and collaboration.

Brook experiences viewed through the perspective of these paradigm shifts allow us to recognize that one season of our life may be over, but God is preparing us for the next season. When I think about Elijah alone with God beside the brook Cherith, I see a man who God was preparing for the next steps in his journey:

Elijah was being prepared to be a house guest and an encouragement to a widow and her son during a season of famine.

Elijah was being prepared to later take on the priests of Baal in the ultimate showdown on Mount Carmel as a prophet and man of God.

Elijah was being prepared to be a mentor and friend to his successor—Elisha.

Finally, Elijah was being prepared to be one of the few persons of faith who would not see death.

Through the deep relationship that He had developed with God, Elijah was taken up to heaven in a whirlwind of fire to be with God.[184]

We can trace the journey of many of the characters mentioned in the Bible through their brook experience to the thing that God was calling them to do next. What lessons did each of them need to learn during the delays in their life that were necessary to prepare them for service? Perhaps Jacob, who had gone through life taking things into his own hands to achieve the outcome he wanted, had to learn once and for all to surrender to God. That night as he wrestled with the Angel, he had to learn that continued trust in his own efforts would get him nowhere. He needed to learn to depend fully on God.[185] It might be that Moses had to learn the patience of a shepherd to be able to lead the rambunctious children of Israel through the wilderness for forty years. Likewise, it is possible that Joseph needed to learn humility or at the very least discretion in how he communicated the gifting in his life. Those many years as a slave no doubt would have had an impact on his view of service. Perhaps, in prison he needed to learn how to rule justly. In sum, there are skills necessary for the next phase of our journey that are best developed through struggle and delay.

But in addition to preparation for service, there is another important aspect of how delays and pain points equip us to serve. Time spent waiting by the brook is a training ground for service, but it can also be a clarifying ground. For example, the disciples experienced deep anguish and grief after Jesus died. In the midst of the emotions of fear about what would happen to them now that their Master had been crucified, they were faced with uncertainties. What should they do next? Should they abandon the faith or should they continue to do the work that Jesus had commissioned them to do? In this waiting spot, based on the time they had spent with Jesus for the previous years and their recollection of the many things He had taught them, the next steps in their journey became clear. They gathered in the upper room waiting for the outpouring of the Holy Spirit that would equip them to do the work necessary to launch the Christian Church. They had gained further clarity about their call to continued service.

The Gift of the Wait

More often than not as we wait on God beside the brook, we end up focusing our attention on the outcome for which we are hoping. What I hope you have come to realize, as I have, is that to focus on the desires of our heart is to miss the point of the wait entirely.

We wait because it is in the waiting that we can get to know God. We wait because it is in the waiting that our character is being developed, strengthened and enriched. We wait because it is the opportunity a gracious God offers us to do the necessary work of aligning everything we are to be in accordance with His will and purpose for our lives.

To focus on the thing we want most as we wait by our brook is to lose sight of the grand prize of the experience; it is to miss out on the real purpose of the wait. The most important thing about the wait is the wait itself! The sum total of our walk with God is to live in the space of waiting *on* and *with* Him. God is so in love with us that he provides us with opportunity after opportunity to connect with Him. He provides opportunities for us to engage in the disciplines that He knows are necessary for us to develop an intimate relationship with Him, to allow Him to heal the sin-disease that affects our character, and to prepare us for meaningful service. It is in the waiting space that we are best positioned to live out our fullest identity in communion with Him and in service to others.

The most important thing about the wait is the wait itself! The sum total of our walk with God is to live in the space of waiting on and with Him.

Chapter 14. Chosen to Wait

About Robins and Eagles

The summer that I observed the robin's eggs in the nest, our family left for an extended road trip en route to Wisconsin for a week-long International Youth Camporee that was sponsored by our denomination. During that week, we camped out in a large airfield with over 50,000 people from almost every country in the world. Every night, we gathered in the open air for an evening worship service. The theme for that year was "Chosen." Through the preaching ministry and a dramatic interpretation, we were reminded of the story of David, chosen and anointed by the prophet Samuel to be king when he was just a boy. It would be many years after that anointing that David would eventually become king. David, like the other Bible characters I have alluded to in this book, navigated brook experience after brook experience in his relationship with God before he was able to wear the crown.

In one of the evening worship segments, the preacher spoke about the longer incubation periods for eagles compared with other birds. I thought it was a fitting illustration of why some brook experiences may last longer than others. I learned that eagles do take a longer time than robins to incubate and leave the nest but for very important reasons. Robins like the American robin have an average wing-span of 14 3/4 - 16 1/2 inches wide,[186] but eagles like the bald eagle have wings that can extend from 5.9 to 7.5 feet wide.[187] Whereas the robin can fly at about 20-36 miles per hour,[188] the bald eagle can clock about

100 miles per hour when diving for prey.[189] Another interesting fact is that robins like most birds fly around 500 feet for most of the year. On the other hand, eagles routinely fly at higher heights. They can reach altitudes of 10,000 feet high.[190] Is it any wonder then that eagles have a longer waiting period to move from hatchling to full adult? Maybe, it is for this reason that the prophet Isaiah says: *"But they that wait upon the Lord shall renew their strength; they shall mount up with wings as eagles."*[191] Those who learn to wait on God, will find the strength they need to soar to great heights—not as robins, but as eagles.

We often equate this mounting up with wings as greater aspirational success—where we finally get the desires of our heart. But I would suggest that to soar at the height of the eagle is to reach an elevated level of spiritual understanding, where we rise above earthly ambitions, where we are able to catch a glimpse of the infinite greatness to which God is calling us. Life challenges and delays in the fulfillment of the things for which we have been praying do not defeat us. They do not weary us. They do not cause us to faint. The brook experience becomes our refueling spot--our energizing spot. From this position, we gain strength to continue. Our spiritual muscles are developed in the context of the waiting relationship with our Creator—God.

The Outcome of the Wait

There are many biblical examples of God answering prayers in the ways that individuals had hoped after a long brook experience. I have highlighted a few in this book. But there are many others. We have the example of King Hezekiah, whom God granted fifteen more years of life,[192] of Jonah being released from a big fish after three days and three nights,[193] and also of Jabez, who asked God to enlarge his territory and God did.[194] For the sisters Mary and Martha, after it seemed like all hope was gone, their prayers that their brother Lazarus would live again were answered in a miraculous way.[195]

However, there are also instances where some others waited on God sometimes in the face of silence, ambiguous outcomes and even the answer "no." I would like to be able to tell you that after many years of waiting, God will grant your persistent prayer request. I cannot. The seven action steps outlined in this book are not the secret code that you need to unlock the door to the thing you most desire. All waiting by the brook experiences do not have a miraculous "yes" ending! The purpose of the wait is not that you get what you want. The gifts of the wait are found in the waiting itself.

I don't know your situation or how God will choose to move. It may be that this book finds you in the midst of your waiting experience wondering if and when God is going to answer your prayers. You may be wondering if God has forgotten you. Perhaps you find yourself like the prophet Elijah waiting for next steps in the midst of an assignment that God has already given; you have been waiting and praying for a long time. It might be that your prayer is like the prayer of Hannah—praying for that long-awaited child. Maybe it is like the prayer of Jacob during the midnight hour; you are still wrestling with God refusing to let go until He blesses you. Perhaps you feel like Joseph that you have been treated unjustly, or like Abraham you are waiting on the promise. Do you find yourself waiting for a miraculous healing like the woman with the issue of blood, or the crippled man beside the pool of Bethesda?[196] Whatever situation you find yourself in, here is what I do know. We can spend much of our Christian life focused on the wrong prize.

We can be like the Samaritan woman at the well asking God to fill our water pot with water from the well, when what God wants to give us cannot be contained in any earthly vessel. It must be contained within us. Jesus finds this woman burdened by circumstances in her life and instead of giving her what she asks for, He gave her something that is more precious—a personal and moving experience with Him at perhaps one of the most distressing times in her life. The woman realizes that the gift is not to be found in the filling of her water pot, but in the infilling of the Spirit of God. She takes that gift and leaves the water pot behind.[197]

A Long-term Relationship

Imagine that two young adults are waiting in the airport for a flight that has been delayed for an hour. They are both eager to get to their destination, so they are disappointed and frustrated that they have to wait. What starts out as an hour delay turns into several hours of further delay, and so their frustration mounts. However, as they sit next to each other in the airport terminal, they begin a conversation. As they talk, they learn that they have much in common. In fact, they are members of the same faith tradition. They have similar career aspirations and ambitions, and mutual life interests. As the delay continues, they decide to have lunch together. After lunch, they continue chatting and learning more about each other; they share stories that provide laugh out loud moments and even talk about their life goals and plans which provide moments of deep reflection and insight for them both.

They are so engrossed in their conversation that they are startled when the flight attendant finally announces that the problem for the delay has been resolved and boarding will begin in the next hour. They realize that their time together is about to come to an end, so they exchange contact information with a promise to continue the communication after this day. The flight attendant makes the boarding call and the flight for which they had long waited is now about to become a reality. Yes, they have finally gotten what they have been waiting for—the departure of their fight—but in the process of waiting they have gained something as well.

Long after the waited for flight, the friendship continues through the years. They are there for each other in some major life moments: they attend each other's wedding; celebrate the birth of each other's children; attend birthday parties and graduation ceremonies; they are shoulders to lean on when life gets difficult; they comfort each other through sickness, death of loved ones, and moments that try them both. And as is the way of all relationships on this side of heaven, they also have some tense moments in their friendship—moments of disagreement and conflict when they almost walk out on the relationship. But they do not. They choose to hold on, and to work through the difficulties because the friendship is too precious, too valuable to them both. Through the ups and downs of it all, the relationship gets stronger, deeper. In fact, they no longer see each other as friends—they see each other as family. That delayed encounter was the beginning of a life enriching and sustaining relational connection.

Continue to Wait

This hypothetical story of strangers meeting at the airport as they wait for an outcome illustrates well how I like to think about my developing relationship with God. When I look back at the grand arc of my life from my first meeting with Him to now, I realize that the best gift was not found in the outcomes for which I had prayed. Rather, the most precious gift has been this deepening relationship that continues even now.

In the same way, whatever your brook experiences, continue to wait *on* and *with* God. He is well worth the wait. Continue to trust the Way Maker. Continue to know that He cares deeply about you. Continue to do what the psalmist urges: "*Wait on the Lord, be of good courage and He will strengthen thine heart.*"[198] He will fulfill His promise and call on your life! He may not fulfill it in the way that you expected, but don't focus on the outcome! Choose to shift your focus away from what you want. Focus instead on the invaluable gifts that are wrapped up in the waiting itself—an intimate relationship with the Maker of the universe that will sustain you through the vagaries of life; a personal journey of spiritual transformation so you can lead your best life here and in the eternal hereafter; and preparation for the work that He is uniquely qualifying you to do in service to others.

Continue to wait on God.

∞∞∞

To soar at the height of the eagle is to reach an elevated level of spiritual understanding, where we rise above earthly ambitions, where we are able to catch a glimpse of the infinite greatness to which God is calling us. Life challenges and delays in the fulfillment of the things for which we have been praying do not defeat us. They do not weary us. They do not cause us to faint. The brook experience becomes our refueling spot--our energizing spot.

Epilogue

Yesterday I left the house for my walk/jog alongside the creek. It is early October and the days are getting shorter now. This morning, I am not alone. My younger daughter, Amya, is with me. I am a bit later than usual. Even though Amya's alarm had gone off, she overslept. Then she had forgotten to lay her clothes out the night before, so we spent a couple of minutes putting together an outfit for her. Finally, I sit in the foyer putting on my shoes, as she runs around trying to find her mask. We finally get going at around 7:30 a.m., and I am more than a bit irritated after waiting.

As the COVID-19 pandemic has continued into fall, many schools have not returned to normal. Amya is with me today because I am now homeschooling her. On Monday and Wednesday mornings I take her with me along the trail as part of our physical education curriculum. On Fridays, Mark takes her out biking. My older daughter's school has also gone online with plans to reevaluate in November about whether they will return to face-to-face instruction. The entire summer has passed with us waiting for the COVID saga to be over, yet it continues.

But now as we walk along the trail, we notice that change is all around us. The leaves are beginning to turn beautiful yellows, reds, and oranges, and the days are getting colder. There are more and more leaves along the path each day, and the soft squish they made under our feet a few days ago has been replaced by more of a crackle as the bright colors have faded to brown. The geese and mallards are gone, but we see a few squirrels scurrying to and fro gathering acorns in preparation for winter. Amya points out a grey catbird almost hidden in the undergrowth quietly taking a sip of water. We stop for a bit to take a photo with my phone. Things are changing all around us, and yet the creek continues along at its usual pace.

As we walk along alternating walking with jogging, Amya and I play a game of asking each other questions in turn. It is a good way to pass the time, and I am learning so much about her through her thoughtful questions and answers. This morning, when it is my turn to respond, she asks me the question I have been silently asking myself over and over for the last several months:

"Mommy, how is the book coming along?"

I pause for a minute, giving myself time to think. "Well," I say to her, "I am revising, and there is still a lot more work to do on it."

Then I confess to her that with my work responsibilities as a professor and co-chair of my department as well as home-schooling, it has been difficult to set aside time to get it done. I have not been as disciplined as I needed to be in the last few months in continuing to get up earlier in the morning to write.

"But I am determined to finish it," I say.

Even as I say this, I feel disappointed in myself. All around me, changes are taking place: in nature, in the way we have ad-justed our lives during this time to work differently, do school differently, and even do church differently. Yet I find myself in this position still beside the brook where our house is nestled in the woods and continuing this almost daily ritual of walking and jogging alongside the creek. Even though I can see now how all of my past brook experiences have positioned me right now, right here beside this brook with an unfinished book, I am still not quite clear about the assignment God has for me next.

I am lost in my thoughts, but I stop mid-stride when Amya asks.

"Mommy, so what are *you* going to do when the book *is* finished?"

We stand there for a bit waiting in the middle of the ques-tion.

"I am not quite sure what is next of me, sweetheart," I say. "But I know Someone who does."

"Let's keep on walking."

Notes

Prologue

1. Kathy-Ann C. Hernandez, "Value What Matters," 2017, https://www.facebook.com/valuewhatmatters.

Chapter 1

2. Jeremiah 28:11.

3. 1 Kings 17:1 (King James Version).

4. 1 Kings 15:34 (KJV).

5. 1 Kings 16:30 (KJV).

6. 1 Kings 16:32-33 (New King James Version).

7. M. G. Easton, Easton's Bible Dictionary, version 2.0 (Albany, OR: Book of the Ages, 1997), http://www.ntslibrary.com/PDF%20Books/Eastons%20Bible%20Dictionary.pdf.

8. 1 Kings 17: 2-3 (KJV).

9. 1 Kings 17: 8-9 (KJV).

10. 1 Kings 17:14 (New Living Translation).

Chapter 2

11. See James 5:17.

12. M. G. Easton, Easton's Bible Dictionary, version 2.0 (Albany, OR: Book of the Ages, 1997), http://www.ntslibrary.com/PDF%20Books/Eastons%20Bible%20Dictionary.pdf.

13. Psalm 27:10 (NLT).

14. Psalm 27: 14 (KJV).

15. Albert Barnes, "Notes on the Bible," accessed October 24, 2020, https://sacred-texts.com/bib/cmt/barnes/index.htm.

16. 2 Samuel 12-16-18 (NLT).

17. 1 John 5: 14-15 (The Amplified Bible).

18. Colin Smith, "When God Hides You," Unlocking the Bible, December 4, 2018, https://unlockingthebible.org/sermon/when-god-hides-you/.

19. Smith, "When God Hides You."

20. 1 Kings 18: 45 (NLT).

21. 1 Kings 19:5 (NLT).

22. 1 Kings 19:11-13 (NLT).

Chapter 3

23. 2 Kings 2:11 (NKJV).

24. Enid Mary Blyton was a very prolific British author of stories, poemsplays, and educational books for children.

25. Kathy-Ann C. Hernandez, "Standing in the Motherhood Gap," Medium (Journal of Journeys, May 11, 2020), https://medium.com/journal-of-journeys/standing-in-the-motherhood-gap-be099e11d72d.

26. See Judges 6:33-40.

27. See Ephesians 3:20.

28. Hebrews 4:11(NLT).

29. Derek Prince and Ruth Prince, God Is a Matchmaker: Seven Biblical Principles for Finding Your Mate (Ada, MI: Chosen Books, 2011).

30. Genesis 2:23 (New International Version).

Chapter 4

31. See Exodus 4:1-10.

32. Mark Batterson, Whisper: How to Hear the Voice of God (Colorado Springs, Colorado: Multnomah, 2020).

33. Batterson, Whisper, 9-10.

34. See 1 John 5:14-18 (NKJV).

35. Daniel 10:1-14 (NLT).

36. Daniel 10:13 (NLT).

37. Psalm 51.

38. Genesis 50: 20 (The Message).

39. 1 Kings 17: 6 (NLT).

40. 1 Kings 17:12 (NLT).

41. Psalm 37: 25 (NIV).

42. 2 Timothy 4:13 (NLT).

43. Matthew 4:1 (NLT).

44. Matthew 26:36–46.

45. Exodus 2:11–7:7, Moses was about 40 years old when he left Egypt, and Exodus 7:7 tells us that he was about 80 years old when he returned from Midian to speak with Pharaoh.

46. Acts 9:10-19.

47. Galatians 1:12 (NIV).

Chapter 5

48. Stephen R. Covey, The 7 Habits of Highly Effective People: Powerful Lessons in Personal Change (New York, NY: Simon & Schuster, 1990).

49. Isaiah 43:19 (KJV).

50. See Isaiah 43:19 (NLT).

51. Hebrews 12:11 (NIV).

52. Richard Lovelace, "To Althea, from Prison," The Oxford Book of English Verse, 1993, https://www.bartleby.com/101/348.html.

53. Luke 2:46-48 (NIV).

54. See Matthew 4:1-11.

55. Philippians 4:11 (KJV).

56. Ephesians 4:20 (NKJV).

57. Jeremiah 29:11 (NIV).

58. Genesis 11:31-32.

59. Philippians 4:13, (NKJV).

60. Genesis 2:15, 2:20.

61. Genesis 30:25-37.

62. John 2:1-12.

63. John 2:11-1.

64. 1 Kings 17:8-16.

65. T.D Jakes, Soar!: Build Your Vision from the Ground Up (Lebanon, IN: Faithwords, 2017).

66. Hebrews 11:1 (NIV).

Chapter 6

67. This is an allusion to what Jesus told Peter. See Matthew 16:13-17.

68. Elisabeth Kubler-Ross, On Death and Dying: What the Dying Have to Teach

Doctors, Nurses, Clergy and Their Own Families (New York, NY: Scribner, 2014).

69. Margaret Stroebe, Henk Schut, and Kathrin Boerner, "Cautioning Health-Care Professionals," OMEGA - Journal of Death and Dying 74, no. 4 (2017): 455-473, https://doi.org/10.1177/0030222817691870.

70. 1 Thessalonians 5:16 (Berean Study Bible).

71. Romans 8:28.

72. John 11:1-44.

73. John 11:1-44.

74. John 9:6.

75. Mark 5: 22-24; 38-43 (NIV).

76. Isaiah 53:3-4 (KJV).

Chapter 7
77. Genesis 32:9 (NLT).

78. Genesis 32:22-31.

79. Ellen G. White, The Story of Patriarchs and Prophets: the Conflict of the Ages illustrated in the Lives of Holy Men of Old (Mountain View, CA: Pacific Press Pub. Assn., 1913).

80. See Hosea 12:4.

81. Genesis 32: 26 (NKJV).

82. Romans 8:26.

Chapter 8
83. 1 Samuel 1:13.

84. Samuel 1:18 (NLT).

85. See Matthew 26:36-46.

86. For example, see Psalm 12.

87. For example, see Psalm 13.

88. Bruce M. Metzger and Michael D. Coogan, The Oxford Companion to the Bible (Oxford: Oxford University Press, 1993).

89. Psalm 6:6 (NIV).

90. Psalm 71:12 (NIV).

91. Psalm 86:12 (NIV).

92. 2 Corinthians 12: 1-10.

93. 2 Samuel 12:17-19.

94. Genesis 32:22-32.

95. A Pyrrhic victory is defined as a victory that has taken such a heavy toll on the victor that it is as good as a defeat. The term itself is an allusion to Pyrrhus of Epirus, who triumphed against the Romans in the Battle of Asculum in 279 BC. But this victory also destroyed much of his forces, and ultimately forced the end of his campaign.

96. Romans 8:28 (NLT).

97. Sonja Lyubomirsky, The How of Happiness: A Practical Guide to Getting the Life You Want (London: Piatkus, 2013).

98. Harvard Health Publishing, "Giving Thanks Can Make You Happier," Harvard Health, accessed October 27, 2020, https://www.health.harvard.edu/healthbeat/giving-thanks-can-make-you-happier.

99. Lyubomirsky, The How of Happiness: A Practical Guide to Getting the Life You Want.

100. John Milton, Paradise Lost, bk. 1, lines 233-234.

101. Matthew 5:45 (NLT).

102. Revelation 4:8 (NIV).

103. Psalm 34:1.

104. James 1: 2 (NLT).

105. "Theology of Joy & the Good Life: YCFC," Yale Center for Faith and Culture at Yale Divinity School, accessed October 27, 2020, https://faith.yale.edu/legacy-projects/theology-of-joy.

106. Miroslav Volf, "The Crown of the Good Life: Joy, Happiness and the Life Well Lived - A Hypothesis," ABC Religion & Ethics (Australian Broadcasting Corporation, August 20, 2015), https://www.abc.net.au/religion/the-crown-of-the-good-life-joy-happiness-and-the-life-well-lived/10097970.

107. Mandisa, "A Broken Hallelujah," Amazon (Balboa Press, 2017), https://www.amazon.com/Broken-Hallelujah/dp/B001VFYFNG.

Chapter 9

108. Genesis 30:22 (NLT).

109. Genesis 37:3 (NLT).

110. Genesis 37:4 (NLT).

111. Genesis 39:2 (NLT).

112. Genesis 39:21 (NLT).

113. Proverbs 22:29 (NLT).

114. Genesis 40:1-20.

115. Genesis 40:25 (NLT).

116. Bayles, Dallyn Vail. Better than I. CD. Shadow Mountain, 2008.

117. Hamlet, Act 5, Scene 2.

118. Ellen G. White, The Story of Patriarchs and Prophets: the Conflict of the Ages Illustrated in the Lives of Holy Men of Old (Mountain View, CA: Pacific Press Pub. Assn., 1913), 219.

119. Daniel 6:3 (KJV).

120. Ecclesiastes 9:10 (NIV).

121. During this time, I became one of the section editors for the book, Diversity Matters: Race, Ethnicity, and the Future of Christian Higher Education. Abilene, TX: Abilene Christian University Press, 2017.

122. Kathy-Ann C. Hernandez, "Valuewhatmatters," Valuewhatmatters, accessed October 29, 2020, https://valuewhatmatters.com/.

123. Exodus 9:1 (KJV).

124. Exodus 2 & 3.

125. Luke 1:80.

126. Matthew 4:1.

Chapter 10

127. 1 Samuel 17:18.

128. See 1 Samuel 17:32.

129. 1 Samuel 30:1-4 (KJV).

130. This was Job's wife's advice to him during his time of suffering. See Job 2:9.

131. Psalm 121:1-2 (NIV).

132. Psalm 23:4 (KJV).

133. Psalm 91:7 (NIV).

134. Psalm 34:1 (KJV).

135. 1 Samuel 30:8, (NLT).

136. 2 Samuel 1:10, (NIV).

137. Donald S. Whitney, Spiritual Disciplines for the Christian Life (Colorado Springs, CO: NavPress, 2014), 4.

138. Luke 5:16 (NIV).

139. Mark 1:35 (NIV).

140. Matthew 14:23, (NIV).

141. See Luke 10:38-42.

142. Jeremiah 1:5 (NIV).

143. Luke 12:7 (English Standard Version).

144. 2 Corinthians 6:18 (NIV).

Chapter 11

145. Luke 8: 43-48.

146. Matthew 9:20-22, Mark 5:25-34, Luke 8:43-48.

147. Leviticus 20:18.

148. Leviticus 15:25-33.

149. Al Woods, "The Woman with the Issue of Blood – 12 Study Points," Homewords Ministry, April 29, 2016, https://homewordsministry.wordpress.com/2016/04/29/the-woman-with-the-issue-of-blood-12-study-points/.

150. Luke 8:48, (NLT).

151. There are many variations of this saying: "The darkest morning is just before dawn." However, the first person to use this phrase that is recorded in print is the English theologian and historian Thomas Fuller. In his religious travelogue A Pisgah-Sight Of Palestine And The Confines Thereof, 1650, he wrote: "It is always darkest just before the Day dawneth."

152. See Matthew 26:36-46.

153. See Luke 22:42.

154. Exodus 4:10, (NLT).

155. Exodus 14.

156. See Job 1:9-11.

157. Job 13:15, (KJV).

Chapter 12

158. Graft versus host disease can happen during stem-cell transplantation when the donor's T cells (the graft) view the patient's healthy cells (the host) as foreign matter, and begin to attack and damage them.

159. Kathy-Ann C. Hernandez, "About Yesterday," Medium (Journal of Journeys, June 15, 2020), https://medium.com/journal-of-journeys/about-yesterday-addad7c43d1f.

160. 2 Corinthians 1:4 (Berean Study Bible).

161. "Maya Angelou," Encyclopædia Britannica (Encyclopædia Britannica, inc.), accessed October 29, 2020, https://www.britannica.com/biography/Maya-Angelou.

162. "Nelson Mandela," Encyclopædia Britannica (Encyclopædia Britannica, inc.), accessed October 29, 2020, https://www.britannica.com/biography/Nelson-Mandela.

163. "Helen Keller," Encyclopædia Britannica (Encyclopædia Britannica, inc.), accessed October 29, 2020, https://www.britannica.com/biography/Helen-Keller.

164. Andrew Solomon, "How the Worst Moments in Our Lives Make Us Who We Are," TED, accessed October 29, 2020, https://www.ted.com/talks/andrew_solomon_how_the_worst_moments_in_our_lives_ma ke_us_who_we_are?language=en.

165. Andrew Solomon, Far from the Tree: Parents, Children and the Search for Identity (New York: Scribner Classics, 2014).

166. Will Kenton, "Understanding Profit," Investopedia (Investopedia, August 28, 2020), https://www.investopedia.com/terms/p/profit.asp.

167. Mary S. Poplin, Finding Calcutta: What Mother Teresa Taught Me about Meaningful Work and Service (Downers Grove, IL: IVP Books, 2008), 150.

168. Katherine Wolf, Desperate for Jesus 2020, accessed October 29, 2020, https://youtu.be/Nho8w9XSMCc.

169. Katherine Wolf, Jay Wolf, and Joni Eareckson Tada, Hope Heals: a True Story of Overwhelming Loss and an Overcoming Love (Grand Rapids, MI: Zondervan Books, 2020).

170. Katherine Wolf and Jay Wolf, Suffer Strong: How to Survive Anything by Redefining Everything (Grand Rapids, MI: Zondervan, 2020).

171. Katherine Wolf and Jay Wolf, "Our Story," HOPE HEALS, 2019, https://www.hopeheals.com/story.

172. Many variations of this quote exist. However, this variation, "Never doubt in the dark what God told you in the light," appears to have been the original. It has been attributed to V. Raymond Edman, an American minister and author who served as the fourth president of Wheaton College in Illinois from 1941

to 1965.

173. Katherine Wolf, Desperate for Jesus 2020, accessed October 29, 2020, https://youtu.be/Nho8w9XSMCc.

Chapter 13

174. The concrete ceiling is defined as those artificial barriers that exist based on attitudinal or organizational bias that pre . Nehemiah 4:14.

175. Isaiah 29:13 (NIV).

176 . Larnelle Harris, "But God [Music Download]," But God [Music Download]: The   Steeles - Christianbook.com, accessed October 29, 2020,   https://www.christianbook.com/the-steeles/but-god/pd/DL151604-CP?event=CBCER1.

178. 1 Corinthians 9:24-27 (NIV).

179. 1 Timothy 4:7 (NASB).

180. Jan Johnson, Abundant Simplicity: Discovering the Unhurried Rhythms of Grace (Downers Grove, IL: IVP Books, 2011).

181. See Exodus 3.

182. Mark Batterson, Whisper: How to Hear the Voice of God (Colorado Springs, Colorado: Multnomah, 2020), 57.

183. 1 Kings 3:9.

184. 2 Kings 2: 13, (NIV).

185. See Ellen G. White, The Story of Patriarchs and Prophets: the Conflict of the Ages Illustrated in the Lives of Holy Men of Old (Mountain View, CA: Pacific Press Pub.   Assn., 1913), 201.

Chapter 14

186. American Robins: Facts, accessed November 1, 2020, https://journey-north.org/tm/robin/facts_characteristics.html.

187. Anne Marie Helmenstine, "Surprising Facts about the Bald Eagle, Emblem of the U.S.," ThoughtCo, April 2, 2019, https://www.thoughtco.com/bald-eagle-facts-4174386.

188. Helmenstine, "Surprising Facts about the Bald Eagle, Emblem of the U.S."

189. National Eagle Center, "How Fast Can Eagles Fly?," National Eagle Center, accessed November 1, 2020, https://www.nationaleaglecenter.org/avada_faq/how-fast-can-eagles-fly/.

190. "Bald Eagle Facts, Information, and Photos," American Expedition, accessed November 1, 2020, https://forum.americanexpedition.us/bald-eagle-

information-facts-   photos-and-artwork.

191. Isaiah 40:31.

192. 2 Kings 2:20-6.

193. See Jonah 1 & 2.

194. 1 Chronicles 4:9-10.

195. See John 11.

196. See John 5:1-15.

197. See John 4:1-28.

198. Psalm 27:14 (KJV).

Letter to the Reader

Dear Reader,

I am so glad that you decided to purchase and read this book, *Waiting by the Brook: Seven Steps to Deeper Intimacy with God*. I hope that it has been an inspiring read that helps you think about the experience of waiting on God in a more nuanced way. More importantly, I hope that you have been encouraged to continue to wait on God even through the difficult moments in life.

Writing this book took me by surprise; it was totally un-planned. However, in the process of writing it, I began to see a path forward for more publications and resources in this genre. If you are interested in other resources including book discussion questions, book quotes, and upcoming publications, please visit me on the web at Value What Matters.

As an author, I love feedback. It is helpful to know if my work is connecting with readers in the way that I intended. So tell me what resonated with you or what did not. Please also let me if you have suggestions for other topics of interest in the genre of spiritual growth. I'd love to hear from you.

Finally, I need to ask a favor. I would be very grateful if you would post a book review. If you are anything like me when con-sidering whether to buy a book or not, reviews are very helpful in guiding the final decision. You, the reader, have the power to do something I cannot --share your honest opinion about this book from a reader's perspective.

Thank you for reading this book and for considering this request.

With a smile,

Dr. H

Kathy-Ann C. Hernandez

VALUE
WHAT
MATTERS

Made in the USA
Las Vegas, NV
27 March 2024

87843865R00098